Read What These Top Achievers Are Saying About

Taking LIFE Head On!

"Incredible. *Taking LIFE Head On!* is a riveting story that grabs your heart. For anyone that has experienced seemingly insurmountable challenges, this book alters your thinking about what's possible, and teaches you the strategies needed to create the extraordinary life that you've always wanted. Hal's courageous and inspiring story has the power to move us all."

—Jon Vroman
Co-founder, *Front Row Foundation*

"Hal changes lives wherever he goes. His tools of impeccable integrity and a positive focus for the future make an impact at the fundamental level needed for anyone to surpass their boundaries and commit to a new level of leadership. The gift of communication has never found a better or more deserving host than Hal Elrod."

—Jeffrey T. Sooey
President & CEO, *JTS Advisors*

"In *Taking LIFE Head On!* Hal Elrod inspires and empowers you with his story, offers powerful strategies to rapidly transform our lives, to experience new levels of freedom, happiness, and love. If you are ready to change your life, I highly recommend that you read this book!"

—Adel Anwar
Guinness World Record Holder for Memory
British Attorney & CEO

"There are very few individuals on this planet who have the ability to give the perfect meaning to every circumstance. Hal Elrod is one of these people. He has proven that we can control our destiny, our emotions, and our lives. Thank you, Hal, for this book!"

—Jon Berghoff
President, *Global Empowerment Coaching*

"Courage is one of the great virtues missing in our society today, and our young people are in desperate need of courageous role models and mentors. Hal's story is amazing. It is a story of courage that we can all be inspired by."

—Matthew Kelly
NY Time bestselling author, *The Rhythm of Life*

"Having been an elite level athlete for most of my life, I have come across several accomplished individuals, coaches, and athletes who seem to defy the physical and mental barriers of human potential. I truly believe that Hal Elrod is one of the most inspirational and courageous people I have ever met.
His heart, his story, his determination, and his authenticity transcend anything I've ever known to exist in a person. I highly recommend this book and his miraculous story to anyone who wants to live an extraordinary life."

—Callie Withers
Professional Soccer Player, *WUSA*

"I have had the pleasure of knowing Hal Elrod both personally and professionally for the for the last six years. His story is one of the greatest testaments to how all of us can take adversity head on and rise to the top."

—Anthony "AB" Bourke
CEO and President, *Afterburner Seminars*

"*Optimism in action* is how I'd describe Hal's story. He is more than a man with a positive outlook. He is a man who exercises his attitude on a daily basis to bring out success in himself and in others."

—Dave Durand
Author, *Perpetual Motivation*

"A mentor once told me that you are never too young and never too old to achieve greatness in life. Hal is fortunate and blessed to be alive and is using this life as an opportunity to positively impact others to greatness. He is truly passing on the blessing!"

—John Ruhlin
President, *Ruhlin Promotion Group*

"Hal is an amazing human being who has learned many of life's lessons on his own, the "hard" way. People who are wise learn by listening to others' experience. I've definitely gained a deeper sense of positive mindset from Hal, as well as the commitment to never give up, when it comes to having the things that you really want in life!"

—Meg Fritton
Master Coach, *Landmark Education*

"Hal is one of the most unique and talented individuals I have ever met. If you really want to take control of your life and do more of what is really meaningful to you, you will find this book is a great tool for you to improve your business and life."

—Tony Carlston
Owner *C&C Enterprises* **&**
Hall of Fame Member, *Cutco/Vector*

"*Taking LIFE Head On!* is a must read for anyone that has faced adversity. An amazing story and an incredible person that everyone can relate to. Put it on your must read list!"

—Steve Pokrzyk
Market Development Manager, *Vector Marketing*

"I've known Hal for many years. He has the special ability to master the meanings that he puts to the events of his life. *Taking LIFE Head On!* shows you how it's possible to turn what seems to be a tragedy, into a gift."

—Matt Recore
President, *Recore Growth Investments, Inc.*

"*Taking LIFE Head On!* is a true testimonial of Hal's courage and strength. I have applied Hal's principles and strategies in my own life and have experienced tremendous growth, both personally and professionally. This book is a shining star among a universe of motivational books. I highly recommend it to anyone that wants profound and lasting change in their life."

—Dan *"The Car Man"* **Perez**
Fleet/Internet Sales Manager, *Geweke Toyota*

Published by

Yo Pal Hal Companies

Sacramento

www.yopalhal.com

ISBN: 978-0-9790197-0-8

Cover design **by Melody Lambert,** *ML Designs*
Cover photograph by **Paul Lyubezhanin,** *Perfect Angle Photography*
"Yo Pal Hal" Logo artwork by **Jeremy Katen**
Editing Team: **Andy Mannle & Bud Gardner**
Chief Editor: **Sarah Baker Andrus**

Taking LIFE Head On!

The Hal Elrod Story

LOVE the life you have so that you can
CREATE the life of your dreams

by

Yo Pal Hal

DEDICATION

This book is dedicated to all of the people in my life who have loved, supported, and prayed for me.
Without each and everyone one of you, this book—my life—would not be possible.

Acknowledgements

It has been almost seven years since I first dreamt of writing this book and sharing my story with the world, but it wasn't until last year that I committed to the process. Once I fully committed, miracles began showing up in my life. Unknown forces in the universe seemingly came together, sending the right people and resources needed for me to make my dream a reality. It is thanks to the combined efforts, love and support of many extraordinary people that you are reading this today.

My sincere and heartfelt gratitude goes out to...

—Bud Gardner and Andy Mannle—my brilliant editing team. Thanks to your incredible talent and insights my ideas, my story, and my dream have been assembled into this life-changing book.

—Sarah Baker-Andrus, my Chief Editor. As I have told you from the beginning, you are my angel, sent from heaven to bring my story to the world. I couldn't do it without you, and I am eternally grateful for your selfless commitment to the truth.

—Jon Berghoff, for your sales and business coaching. I have never met an individual with such depth and expertise in the area of selling. Your combination of wisdom along with your desire to give back, never stop amazing me. Thank you for your love, insight, and encouragement.

—All of my CUTCO customers. I have learned something valuable from each of you, and it is thanks to your love, loyalty and support that I have been able to create the life I have today.

—My CUTCO/Vector friends, colleagues, managers and executives. You are my second family and have been the greatest influence on my life. You have taught me so much about how to treat people, what is to be valued in business, and how to live with integrity. Thank you!

—Authors, speakers, and mentors such as Wayne Dyer, Neale Donald Walsh, Anthony Robbins, Tim Sanders, Roger Crawford, Matthew Kelly, and Dave Durand for your unwavering commitment to adding value to the lives of others. You have forever changed mine.

—The residents of Oakhurst and surrounding areas. Growing up in our small mountain community was truly a blessing for me. Thank you for your love and support throughout the years.

—Each person who selflessly shared your valuable time and energy to visit me in the hospital. Your energy and love gave me life.

—My best friends—none better than the other—every single one of you is extraordinary. We have created many memories together with so many more to come. I love each of you more than words can ever express, and I am committed to loving and supporting you for the rest of my life and beyond.

—My family—aunts, uncles, cousins, and grandparents—for the immeasurable amount of love that you have always shown me. Some of my greatest memories, spanning from my childhood to now, were created together with you. I love you very much.

—My sister, Hayley, who lives with such remarkable integrity and is constantly adding value to my life through her sisterly advice. Thank you for taking such good care of me, Sis!

—My mom and dad—you are *the best!* You have instilled in me the values that continue to guide me through my life. I love you, and I am blessed to be your son.

Finally, I thank God, my Creator and the Source of all that is, for blessing me with unconditional love and the wisdom to love unconditionally.

CONTENTS

If you want to write to the author, you can visit his website at **www.yopalhal.com**

Foreword

By Bud Gardner

I am in awe of Hal Austin Elrod and his amazing true story. What a fantastic young man he is and what an important book he has written here, which can be a turning point for many unfulfilled lives. His devastating car wreck, his fight to survive, his painful recovery, and his seemingly impossible climb back to the pinnacle of success are all remarkable milestones in rebuilding his life. How many of us have the courage or determination to do that?

Hal could not have done this without his positive, upbeat, unyielding attitude and burning desire to overcome any obstacle put before him. He epitomizes the philosophy set forth in the classic book, *Man's Search for Meaning*, by psychiatrist and author Viktor E. Frankl, who discovered the mystery of why so few prisoners survived German concentration camps in World War II:

"...everything can be taken from a man but one thing: The last of his freedoms—to choose one's attitude in any given set of circumstances, to choose one's own way."

And choose Hal Elrod did. He could have easily given up, but Hal chose otherwise.

At age 20, he had it all. As a distributor for the Cutco knife company, he quickly became one of the best salesmen in Cutco's

50-year history, continuously breaking sales records and setting new standards. He was the pride of the company, constantly mentoring newcomers and giving motivational speeches at company rallies.

Then one fateful night all that changed. After giving a rousing speech, he climbed behind the wheel of his brand new, white Ford Mustang with his girlfriend, Amber, and hit the open road. Moments later, a drunk driver smashed into Hal's car, shattering his world. Then an instant later, a second car plowed into his driver-side door. Hal was found dead at the scene, his girlfriend unconscious. Miraculously, Hal's heart began to beat again; then he slipped into a deep coma. The airbag saved Amber's life.

Eventually, he awoke from the coma, but Hal was not given much hope to live. After eight surgeries and being told by doctors he would not walk for a year, Hal set his mind to prove them wrong. Three weeks later, he took his first step; four weeks later he left the hospital. Eight weeks after the accident, he was back on the job and on stage, again among the top salesmen for Cutco.

Hal Elrod is living proof that all of us are capable of creating miracles in our own lives. And this inspirational book, loaded with examples of Hal's never-say-die attitude and winning strategies, will empower anyone to make the most of his or her life. All you need is a beating heart and a burning passion to conquer *your* world.

Prologue

PRESUMED DEAD

I flashed her a playful, boyish grin, and inserted my new Tchaikovsky CD into the stereo. The powerful orchestra began to fill the cab of my new Ford Mustang, as my girlfriend Amber and I pulled out of the restaurant's parking lot ahead of Jeremy. I accelerated my new thoroughbred through the intersection toward Highway 99, and as I glanced in my rear-view mirror I saw Jeremy get stuck at a red light. *Too bad for him,* I thought.

I swiftly wielded my five-speed transmission through all five gears, Ford's pearl-white pedigree catapulting us onto the freeway and in seconds we were traveling through time and space at a cruising speed of 70 miles-per-hour. My mind was flowing with thoughts of the evening's events. We had such a great night, I wanted to call my mom and dad, at home in Oakhurst to share my excitement, but with a quick glance at the digital display on my dash, the clock warned me that it was approaching midnight, so I decided to wait until morning.

Fifteen miles south of Buck's restaurant, a man whom I had never met was enjoying his Friday night as well. He may have been exhausted, or overly stressed from another long day of work. Whatever the reason, he stopped in to have a few beers at The Atwater Pub before going home. As the barkeeper would later attest, the man had made his routine stop by the bar many nights before and only lived a few miles away. The man hopped into his navy-blue Chevy 4X4 truck and sped out of the parking lot, intending to take his regular route down Highway 99, home to his wife and son. Impaired by the alcohol he had just consumed, he mistakenly turned the wrong direction onto the ramp as he entered the freeway...

I don't know about you, but I love a good action movie—car crashes, explosions, and nonstop thrills—always keep me on the edge of my seat. However, what follows did not take place in the theatre, or at home on the big-screen, this was my real life. Some of it is not easy to tell or comfortable to hear, but all of it is the truth of my story.

I do not recall acknowledging the two headlights coming towards me. After all, this was a trip I had made before, and the last thing I would have imagined is the possibility of headlights appearing right in front of me on the highway—but they did. I don't think my brain was able to accept it as reality, but I cannot tell you that for sure.

In a moment of twisted fate, my new Ford Mustang collided with the Chevy truck at a lethal 70 miles-per-hour. The next few seconds played out in slow motion, Tchaikovsky's commanding melodies orchestrating our wicked dance.

The metal frames of our two vehicles collided—screaming and screeching as they twisted and broke. The airbags of the

Mustang exploded with enough force to knock Amber and me unconscious. And my brain, still traveling at seventy miles-per-hour, smashed into the front of my skull, destroying the vital brain tissue of my frontal lobe.

Upon impact, the tail end of my Mustang was shoved into the lane on my right, my driver's side door placed directly in the path of an oncoming vehicle. A Saturn sedan, keeping pace at over 70 miles-per-hour, crashed into my driver's side door at full force. My door collapsed into the left side of my body, and the frame of the metal roof caved in on me, slicing open my skull and nearly severing my left ear. The bones of my left eye socket collapsed, leaving my left eyeball dangerously unsupported. My left arm broke, severing the radial nerve in my forearm and shattering my elbow, while my fractured humorous bone pierced through the skin behind my bicep.

Given the impossible challenge of separating the Saturn's front end from the center console of my Mustang, was my pelvis, which failed and broke three places. Finally, my femur snapped in half, spearing through the skin of my thigh and tearing a hole in my black dress slacks began flooding the car with my blood.

Unable to withstand the immeasurable pain, my brain shut down, my blood pressure began to drop, and I fell into a coma...

Despite many attempts, I simply cannot remember the shock and pain of my accident. I only know the details recited above from talking with friends and family, listening to my doctors, and reading police reports.

Since my accident I have learned many remarkable lessons, most of which I never would have put in a request for, but I was not given the luxury of choosing. I was, however, not entirely without choice. The choice that I had is the same choice that you have everyday of your life, and that is to choose our response to any situation—good or bad—that we are faced with. On the one hand, I could have chosen to be a victim, dwelling on the negative aspects of my circumstances, feeling sorry for myself, and indulging in the sorrow that everyone felt for me... On the other, I could choose to be grateful for my life, focus my energy and attention on what I could control in creating the circumstances I wanted, and help other people through my experience.

To *LOVE & CREATE*... this is the essence of life. And I continue to learn that no matter how difficult life's challenges may seem at any given moment, the choice is always available for us *to LOVE the life we have so that we can CREATE the life of our dreams.* Anything you dream—if you believe and commit to it—you can create it. This is not just true for some people; it is absolutely true for all of us.

The accident was just one of many difficult events in my life, and I'm sure you, too, have endured your share. This book certainly was inspired by my response to the tragic events that occurred on that December evening, but there have been other moments of overwhelming adversity, times when life just seemed really hard or exceedingly unfair. There have been days when giving up was all that I thought I had the strength for, and yet I am still here.

It is my hope that by reading my story you will see that if I can do it, then so can you. Since I could genuinely *love the life I had*, even in the midst of some of the most painful and difficult circumstances you can imagine, then that same choice is available to you in your everyday life. And making the conscious choice to *create the life of my dreams* is something I am constantly choosing in each moment of every day. You too can make that choice in your life. I hope you will choose to learn from the strategies that my family and I have used to turn our tragedies into triumphs, and find ways to apply them in your own life immediately.

Human beings are capable of crazy, ridiculous, marvelous, miraculous things! They run literally all night long, build enormous stone structures with their hands, create beautiful works of art, survive cancer, write ballads, fight fires, skydive, and die for each other. They strap themselves to rockets and explode into the atmosphere—why wouldn't you and I be able to create extraordinary lives for ourselves? Why is it that when a baby is born we refer to that as the *miracle of life*, but then we go on to complain about our own lives? Where along the way did we lose sight of the miracle that *we are living*?

Taking Life Head On means choosing every day to LOVE *the life you have* and taking consistent action *so that you can*

CREATE the life of your dreams. It is about being the designer of your life, and not a victim of your circumstances. And it begins the moment you start living every day like your life depends on it. The moment you accept responsibility for *everything* in your life is the moment you unleash the power to create *anything* in your life. It is then that you become empowered to *LOVE the life you have so that you can CREATE the life of your dreams.* It is time to start living *every day* like your life depends on it... because it does.

I am living proof that no matter how difficult things may seem—even in the midst of the most unimaginable pain and tragedy—there is always hope, and we always have the power to *create* anything we want in our lives. Whether your struggles are life threatening as mine were, or simply difficult, you and I share the same unstoppable human spirit. It is my commitment to you that this book will help you appreciate the miracle of your life every day, while designing the future of your dreams.

This book is full of personal stories, factual experiences, empowering strategies and some profound lessons that I have learned. My intention is that my story will empower you to *LOVE the life you have so that you can CREATE the life of your dreams*—and to get started right away. In other words... I wrote this book for *you.*

If you advance confidently in the direction of your dreams and endeavor to live the life which you have imagined, you will meet with a success unexpected in common hours. You will put some things behind, will pass as invisible boundary; new, universal and more liberal laws will begin to establish themselves around and within you; or the old laws be expanded, and interpreted in your favor in a more liberal sense, and you will live with the license of a higher order of beings...

—HENRY DAVID THOREAU

1

A RUDE AWAKENING

"The sun is always shining on the
other side of our clouds."

—Jon Berghoff

I came into the world on May 30th, 1979—three weeks late, weighing a solid nine pounds, seven ounces, and already a force to be reckoned with. My head was so large that the doctors wanted to use forceps to pull me out, but my mom said *no*, that she could do it on her own, and she did. I was the largest baby at the hospital that day, and the staff dubbed me *Big Hal*. I was named after my mom's father, who died just three months after I was born. Everyone who knew him said that I was a lot like my grandfather: ornery and full of *spit and vinegar.*

My name is Hal Elrod. My friends and colleagues call me *Yo Pal Hal,* which I will explain later. It is my sincere belief that you and I have a lot in common, because at the most fundamental physical and spiritual level, we are the same. We are human. Each day, striving to find our purpose, we fight that same fight—the fight to be whole, to be a better person, to do what we know is right—the human fight.

As human beings we share the human experience—common mental and emotional challenges. I used to wake up every day with the fear that I wasn't good enough, that I might fail at life. I used to question my place in the world and what my purpose was. There was a time when I lived my life from a place of fear and inadequacy.

I am as average as the next guy, and as normal as any of us would consider ourselves; just an ordinary person. However, I have been blessed—some might say cursed—with unimaginable adversities, which have provided me with both the challenge, and the opportunity, to *LOVE the life I have* so that I could learn what I needed to know in order to *CREATE the life of my dreams*. Through it all, I have learned a great deal about fulfilling the potential that is within all of us; it is to empower you to realize and achieve your own potential, and to *CREATE the life of YOUR dreams*, that I am writing this to you now.

Prior to my accident, I was young, naïve, and full of confidence—a confidence that ran only as true and as deep as the inadequacies I was covering up.

Like most children, I don't remember my toddler years, so let me begin where my memory will allow, for though the accident was a defining moment in my life, it does not define me as a person. Raised in the small town of Oakhurst, California (near Yosemite National Park), I had a youth filled with fun times, friends, and, like many young boys, the occasional mayhem.

When I was in sixth grade my family purchased a grocery store. The Oakhurst Market was built in 1945, and we lived in a three-bedroom apartment built on top of the store. This provided for all kinds of unique experiences, the most basic being that my sister, Hayley, and I were able to step out of our living room and grab groceries off the shelf—even in our pajamas. It was like having our very own 3,000 square foot pantry. Frequently, when our friends stayed over, we would even use the space as a private after-hours roller skating rink.

I often found myself in trouble as a preteen. I was mischievous; not malicious or mean-hearted; I just tended to act first and think later. Sound familiar? I was a very hyperactive child, which presented many challenges to my parents and teachers. No matter the age though, there is one thing about me that has always been true: my general fearlessness, a trait that would prove to be very useful.

Though I am not one to make excuses, some of my problems as a child may have come from attention-deficit/hyperactivity disorder (AD/HD). AD/HD is a behavioral disorder affecting children and adults that is characterized by problems with attention and impulsivity. Unfortunately, this condition would often get in the way of clear thinking, clouding my judgment and decisions. While I wasn't diagnosed until my early twenties, over the years I have been able to learn more about the condition and find productive ways of dealing with it.

On the road to becoming an adult, two life-altering events impacted my existence. The first was arguably the worst day of my life, and the other I remember as my best day ever. It is strange how people usually do not realize they are having the best day of their lives until that day has come and gone.

However, lots of us convince ourselves that we are having the worst day of our life when we actually have no idea how bad things could really get. Isn't that how life seems to be for most people? It always seems to be easier to recognize the negative than the positive.

Unfortunately, not all people are emotionally prepared to handle tragedy. In life, there are those who let tragedy ruin their lives and everything that they stand for, while others somehow find the strength and emotional fortitude to overcome tragedy. These people find proactive reasons within the context of life's events, which empower them to be stronger and prepare them for their next challenge. One August morning, in 1987, would teach me which person my mom was.

I was lying in bed, in a deep restful sleep, when suddenly I was woken by my mother's screams. My mind was foggy, and trying hard to make sense of the situation, I focused my attention and forced myself to wake up. I heard my mom crying out from across the hall. For a moment, I thought my mom was playing with my baby sister, so I rolled over to go back to sleep.

Then she cried out again. This time, there was no mistaking the fear and urgency in her voice. The sound of her anguish woke me again, and I sensed something was seriously wrong. I jumped out of bed and rushed to my mother's bedroom, where I found her clutching my baby sister, Amery, and breathing into her mouth.

"Mommy, what's going on?" I asked, still wearing my pajamas, not fully aware of the gravity of the situation.

I know now that Mom had noticed Amery was somewhat listless the previous day. She tried to get an appointment down in the valley with Amery's pediatrician, but they couldn't take her until the next day. So, still concerned she brought Amery to the local doctor who didn't know much about Amery's condition (Amery was born with dwarfism). He dismissed my mother's concerns and Amery's symptoms as a "common cold." In fact, Amery was suffering from heart failure, and it's likely nothing would have saved her that morning. Mom had just finished nursing Amery, who was about a year old, and was singing a lullaby when Amery's eyes went blank and my mother felt the life go out of her.

As I walked into the room, my mother looked up at me. She was short of breath, and cried out with unbridled panic, "Hal, oh Hal. Amery's not breathing. We have to call 9-1-1; call 9-1-1!"

I was only eight years old at the time and did not fully comprehend what was happening. My sister was lying there, motionless, with no expression on her face and a blank stare in her eyes. I looked at her for what seemed like an eternity, trying to make sense of what was going on, when my mother spoke again, this time with a calmer and more direct tone, geared to get my complete attention. "Hal, the phone is in the living room. Please call 9-1-1. Tell them Amery's not breathing!"

My mother pulled herself to her feet like a soldier who was not going to give up. Amery was gripped tight in her arms. Looking over toward me, Mom spoke once more, this time with clear instructions, "Come on, Hal, the phone is in the living room."

Coincidently, just a few weeks earlier my mom had taken an adult and infant CPR course that had been offered at the phone company where she worked. So, as she began CPR on Amery, she handed me the phone and sternly said, "Call 9-1-1, Hal. Call 9-1-1!"

This time, her words drove me into action, and I quickly pressed the button that called the fire department, police and ambulance. A woman answered and I told her that my sister was not breathing. She asked many specific questions, and I was forced to relay them to my mother who was still attempting to give my sister mouth-to-mouth resuscitation. My mom was short of breath and I was limited by my age, so this was a painfully long process. Finally, I conveyed all of the pertinent information to the woman and she assured me that an ambulance was on its way. Gripped with fear, I looked down at my mother who was still trying endlessly to breathe life into my sister.

At eight, I knew that Amery was born with a "special" heart and it required her to spend a lot of time at the children's hospital. I wondered if something was wrong with her heart, and maybe that's what was happening. After a few moments, my mom looked up at me, breathing heavily, and instructed me to run to our neighbor Grant's house. "Grant has an oxygen mask... quick, Hal... go tell Grant that Amery's not breathing and to bring his oxygen mask!" she shrieked.

I stood for a second and after registering what she had said, I ran out the front door, running across our deck and over the path of fallen pine needles to Grant's house. Finally, I felt as if I could be of use, that I could have a helping role in saving my baby sister. I stopped suddenly as I arrived at my destination and banged loudly on Grant's bright yellow front door screaming, "Grant! Open the door... please... open your door, Grant!" I continued banging until our 70-year-old neighbor finally managed to reach the front door.

As the door opened inward, I swallowed my fear down hard and explained that my mother needed oxygen because Amery was not breathing. Grant looked for a moment as if he had suffered a heart attack of his own. "What? Amery's not breathing! Well, hold on just a minute I've got it right over here," he exclaimed, wanting to help. "You stay put Hal, I'll go get it." In what seemed like the slowest possible motion, the old man turned and shuffled across the floor to his recliner where his oxygen had been carefully tucked away. As swiftly as his aged bones would let him, he brought the oxygen to the front door. Without hesitation, I grabbed his arm tightly and urged him to get moving. Grant and I hurried out onto the deck that led to his yard, and then we scurried across my front yard and through the front door of my house, which was left wide open just as I had left it.

When we arrived, we found my mom crouched on the floor still trying desperately to breathe life into Amery. She looked up at us as Grant knelt down with his portable oxygen tank in hand, placing the mouthpiece over Amery's tiny lips.

"Here ya go, Amery," he whispered as he turned the metallic knob to release the flow of oxygen. Unfortunately the mouthpiece was designed for an adult-sized mouth. It was far too large for Amery, and the oxygen blew past her pale cheeks. Feeling helpless, Grant started mumbling, "It's too big, the mouthpiece is just too big."

I too felt helpless as I watched this horrific scene play out before me. I remember searching my thoughts, wondering what I could do to help. Finally, I looked at my mother and asked her if I should do the only other thing I could think of that might possibly help, "Mommy, should I pray?"

"Yes, Hal, please pray," she whispered out with an utter hopelessness I did not notice then, but can recall so vividly now. That second, I knelt down on my knees and prayed aloud with all of my heart and soul for God to save my precious sister.

Just then, with my lips mumbling my rapid prayers, as many as I could fit between each breath, I heard the ambulance sirens off in the distance. "Mommy, mommy, I hear the ambulance!" My eyes were wide as I shouted with a growing excitement at the salvation soon to come. I looked down at my sister on the floor and it sent shivers down my spine. It was then when I looked at her blank stare that I understood a little bit better what truly was going on.

The first emergency person to arrive was a member of the local sheriff's department and he immediately took over administering CPR to my little sister. Just then, I heard some loud clumping and ran to the rectangular window next to the front door to see two men carrying what looked like heavy medical equipment. They rushed in and asked my mother what had happened. She frantically attempted to give them a complete summary of the events of the terrifying morning, when she finally fell short of breath and fainted. One of the men caught her before her body slumped to the ground, as the other one dropped to his knees to help Amery.

Grant stood on the side and offered information when asked, while I stood there alone, feeling absolutely helpless. Unable to control my emotions any longer, I started screaming for my mother. The medics were able to quickly revive her, and after helping me calm down, she tried to track down my dad who had been working two jobs at the time. "Mark, Amery stopped breathing," she cried helplessly, hoping to pull from his strength through the phone lines. "We called 911 and the sheriff is giving her CPR. The ambulance is here and they're going to take her to Oakhurst Hospital." She had tears running down her face and I felt so sad. I thought of my other sister, Hayley, who was staying with my grandma for the summer. I wished so bad that she were here with me. After a few seconds of silence, Mom spoke once more into the handset with a sliver of emotion that defines the human spirit... hope. "Okay, I'll do that," she replied to my dad, "We'll meet you at Urgent Care."

She began calling her friends in hopes of finding someone to watch me while she rode in the ambulance with Amery.

Shortly thereafter, her close friend Janine arrived at the house. She spoke briefly with my mother, gave her a hug, wiped away a tear and joined me on the couch. My mother hugged me tightly, assured me it was going to be okay, and then walked out to the ambulance. The flashing red lights turned on as my mom drove away with my sister.

Janine took me to her house where her two sons, Ben and Andy, were waiting. Ben was in my class, and his brother Andy was one grade below us, plus we knew each other from church.

We played with toys and kept ourselves busy while Janine sat quietly at the kitchen table. After about an hour, the phone rang. Janine answered and told me that it was my dad and to go pick up the phone in her bedroom. I made my way down the hall and picked up the receiver off the nightstand. "Hi Dad. Is Amery okay?"

I had never heard my dad cry before, and he was doing his best to be strong for me, but I could feel the sadness in his voice. He struggled to get the words out, "Amery is in heaven."

Being only eight years old, I did not know how to respond to this news, internally nor on the outside. The emotion contorting my face was of sadness and misunderstanding. "She died?"

My dad sobbed, "Yes, but it's going to be okay, Hal. Don't worry, we'll be okay. I love you, Hal."

"I love you too, Dad."

My father told me to give the phone to Janine and said that he would have her bring me to the hospital to see Amery. I set the receiver down on the nightstand and walked slowly into the living room, dragging my feet, and trying to think of what to say when I got there. As I entered into the living room, Janine stood with her arms by her side and a look of sincere grief on her face. Ben and Andy also stared at me, as everyone waited to hear what I had to say. I felt lost, lonely, and afraid, and I didn't like the feeling. Instantly, I perked up and smiled.

"Guess where Amery is...? She's up in heaven!" I proclaimed as if I were announcing a trip to Disneyland.

Janine's bottom lip began to quiver and a tear streaked down her cheek. "Hal, I'm so sorry. Are you okay?"

"Yeah, I'm fine," I said matter-of-fact. "My dad wants to talk to you though."

I had not really understood what death and sadness were about until that day. My parents were sad, undoubtedly so, but they were also strong. It was that strength which made the difference and allowed us to deal with the event in the best possible way. As I can recall, this was the worst day of my life, but it was that day when I learned what kind of family I had, and the type of people my parents were.

My family mourned Amery's loss every day, but we stuck together and we grew stronger. Years later my mother told me what the scene was like that day at the hospital. She said that she remembered seeing Amery's bare chest hooked up with electrodes and her skin was soaking wet. She had thought that perhaps an IV had come loose, but then noticed that Amery was not covered in some foreign liquid, but it was the tears of the nurses and doctors who had worked to save her life. Many of those doctors and nurses attended Amery's funeral, as did an array of strangers from the community who had seen Amery around town, or been touched by her special smile.

I keep this story tucked away in my heart even today and appreciate the support from all of those involved. But no support was greater than that of my parents, who could have easily turned this situation into an excuse to give up on their life and dreams. Instead of becoming victims of tragedy, my parents decided to ask themselves empowering questions, which allowed them to find peace as well as empowering reasons for why this had happened: *How can I learn from this experience?* and *How can I use this experience to help others?* With the answers to their questions came their salvation; they found peace and a sense of purpose.

Right away my mom began reading books on the subjects of death, dying, and grief. Two weeks after Amery's passing, my mother attended her first *Compassionate Friends* meeting. Compassionate Friends is a support group for bereaved parents. Coincidently, the meetings that were to help my mom deal with Amery's death were held at Saint Agnes hospital, which was the same hospital that Amery was born in. One year after attending her first meeting, my mother founded her own bereaved-parents-support-group in our hometown of Oakhurst, which she continued to lead for the next 10 years.

That very next spring, my mom and dad brought to Oakhurst the *Kid's Day* fundraiser for Valley Children's Hospital. Valley Children's is the hospital where Amery received most of her exceptional care and treatment during her time alive. Our entire family—my parents, grandparents, aunts, uncles and cousins—all sold newspapers on one designated day each year to raise money for the hospital.

My family and I did grieve Amery's death, as that is the natural human reaction to loss. Yet despite our crushed expectations and sorrow, we put the energy that we had toward helping those less fortunate by developing initiatives that would empower others. Helping others grow stronger made us grow stronger too. My parents are true pillars of strength and taught me what it means to give selflessly to others.

My parents also taught me that it is my responsibility to find the good in every situation—that it is not what happens to us that matters so much as it is how we respond that determines our lives. In Amery's death and by the will of my parents, I learned that no matter the tragedy, we can find good in every experience. The good that we find in every situation is like the sun; it is always shining on the other side of our clouds, our pain—we just have to *remember* that it's always there for us to find.

We cannot always control what causes us pain, but we can always control our attitude and how we respond to what happens to us. Our pain disappears the moment we find something to be grateful for, even within the context of what is causing us pain. Our gratitude may come from lessons we choose to learn, or from some action that we can take that may add value to our life or the lives of others.

It is my sincere hope that you never have to go through a moment as I did with Amery's death. Though in all honesty, you will likely feel some deep burning pain at some point in your life, a pain that goes beyond the everyday problems of a failed relationship or futile work experience. When that pain comes, I sincerely hope you do not have a second event beset you such as the car accident I lived through. But, if fate does choose you, I want you to realize that you do have the strength to overcome any challenges that come your way, the choice to genuinely love the life you have and the passion to create the life of your dreams.

2

YOUTH, FRIENDSHIP, AND BETRAYAL

"If you want children to keep their feet on the ground, put some responsibility on their shoulders."

—Abigail Van Buren

By the time I hit my teenage years, I thought I was well on my way to becoming an adult. I imagine this is the case for most adolescents, but in my mind, in my world... I just *knew*.

Even at a young age, I knew that I wanted to be independent and to be my own man. When I was twelve, I started working 20 hours a week in my parent's grocery store to help out and earn money. I was not deprived by any means, nor was I a victim of child labor; I was simply interested in making my own money and was willing to work for it.

I also had an entrepreneurial spirit and had developed a love for music at an early age, so when I was fifteen, my best friend Jake and I began our own mobile DJ service. It was so successful that I was given the opportunity to host my own radio show at 16.

At the time I was not aware that I was doing anything "special" or out of the ordinary; I was just pursuing something that I was genuinely excited about. DJing was a blast and I could make money doing it. This simplistic view set the groundwork for my desire to always do what I love, and love what I do.

I attended Yosemite High for high school, where I developed strong relationships with friends and mentors. I had some very encouraging teachers that made me fall in love with learning without me even realizing it. Though education never really came easily for me, it was in the realm of relationships where I would most often struggle.

For me specifically, the problem was that, despite my parents' efforts to teach me the value of giving, I didn't apply it to my own personal life. I was selfish. With strangers I would be the most giving person in the world, helping others while trying to learn from their experiences. However, with those close to me, it was a completely different story.

With relationship after relationship, I always found myself taking more than I gave. I would often volunteer my time to raise money for the Children's Hospital and many other worthy causes. However, when it came to the loved ones around me, I often found that it was *all about me*, and I would not give their needs or wants a second thought at all. In general, I was somewhat self-centered.

A humorous example of this aspect of my personality was when I used to tell people that I thought the best soccer team would be one that was made up of nine *Hals*. Then I would do my brief monologue of what this team would be like: *"Hal passes the ball to Hal—who dribbles down the field and finds Hal open near the net. Hal kicks it high in the air toward the goal as Hal runs into position, and as Hal shoots, Hal scores!"*

It was all in fun, but enough to make you want to throw up. My mom still teases me about this story to this day.

Despite my problems with being selfish, I did have a few close friends in school. My two best friends at Yosemite High were Jacob Williams and Brian Bedel. Jake and I were best friends and we spent most of our time outside of school hanging out together. I could always count on Brian to stand by me, especially on those days when the school bullies picked on us. Unfortunately, this was most days.

One regular such occurrence was when Brian and I were changing after gym class and some seniors would surround us, pick us up fully clothed, and toss us into the running showers. For Brian and me, this kind of hazing happened more often than I now care to admit, but for Jake it was just the opposite. Jake's older brother Kolin watched out for him and kept the bullies away when he was around. Still, Jake and I managed to get ourselves into frequent trouble in and out of school. I'm sure we got each other into more mischief together than either of us ever would have gotten into on our own.

Occasionally, during our freshman year, Kolin would give us a ride in his Volkswagen Bug to go off campus and eat lunch at Danny's Pizza Factory. One day at lunch, I was confronted outside the pizza parlor by one of the school bullies whose nickname was *Spanky*. Spanky lived with his grandmother and accused me of prank calling her house late the night before.

I can honestly tell you I had nothing to do with the call.

However, Spanky did not believe my pleas of innocence and insisted that it was I who made the prank call. I've always been more of a lover than a fighter, so I tried to reason with him and joke my way out of it, but he'd already made his mind up and insisted we fight. A circle of students had formed and his friends were egging him on. My stomach was churning and my heart racing. Then, one of Spanky's friends pointed out, "If you guys fight here, you'll both get suspended. You should fight at the park."

I was scared to death and wanted to avoid this altercation at all costs, but out of fear and peer pressure, I succumbed to his challenge and it was agreed that we would meet over at Oakhurst Park. Everyone scattered throughout the parking lot and hurried to their respective vehicles to make their way over to see the brawl.

Jake and I quickly rushed to Kolin's VW. Once inside, Kolin asked if I was sure I wanted to go to the park. To be honest, I was in complete terror. I was not a fighter—I was the nice, funny, class-clown type—and had never thrown a punch in my life. I really didn't want to fight; I just wanted to go home.

Jake agreed, but for different reasons. He said that it would be a mistake to fight Spanky on his terms and that I should instead fight on my own terms. It would show Spanky that I was in control. Yeah right. Jake then suggested that we should go to their house. Kolin agreed, driving past the turn off for Oakhurst Park, and I breathed a sigh of relief.

When we got to Jake and Kolin's house, I begged Kolin to teach me how to box since he was an avid boxer and had gloves and a heavy bag in the house. I spent the rest of the afternoon taking instruction from Kolin, training on the heavy bag and preparing myself for the seemingly inevitable fate I was sure to face the next day at school. By the end of the day, I had imagined what the fight would be like dozens of times and felt more prepared, but I was still terrified. Fortunately, the opportunity to show Spanky my new skills firsthand never came to fruition, since he got into a fight with another student the next morning on the bus and forgot all about me. Boy was I relieved!

Jake provided more than good brotherly advice—we also started our first business together.

One weekend, Kolin was asked to DJ a school dance at Oakhurst Intermediate Junior High, but a few days before he had to opt out. Always ones to see an opportunity, Jake and I decided to do it. We combined our parents' stereo systems and went to the dance at our old junior high school. Jake played the music, and I was the emcee on the microphone, announcing songs and pumping everyone up. It was a fantastic experience, so great, in fact, that it got me started on my first career path as a DJ.

Unfortunately, the summer after our freshman year, Jake and my friendship came to a dramatic halt. To be honest, it was entirely my fault and is something I regret to this day.

We were at a campground just outside of Oakhurst and Jake

met a girl named Wendy. He was attracted to her right away and expressed to me how much he liked her. Before introducing us, he suggested I tell her that I was 'gay' to lessen the chance that she might fall for me. I gladly played along, and for the next few days we all hung out at the lake together. Jake asked me if I would do him a favor and talk to her, so one day when I was alone with Wendy, I told her about Jake's feelings for her. She said that she liked Jake, but only as a friend. To my surprise, she further added that she did like me and knew that I was not really gay, then leaned in and kissed me. Wendy was hot and I felt the attraction right back.

That was a decisive moment for me. I could do the right thing, respect my best friend and tell Wendy our love was not to be, or I could succumb to my infatuation, throw caution to the wind and try to hide it from Jake for as long as possible. Wendy's beauty and adorable personality did me in.

For the duration of the summer, I hid my relationship with Wendy as we kept seeing each other. Of course, Jake eventually found out and told me that our friendship was over, as was our DJ partnership. He could not believe that I would listen to him talk about Wendy for weeks on end while I was secretly seeing her. I felt horrible about what I had done, and his feelings of betrayal were surely justified.

To make matters worse, as with most high school relationships, love is fleeting. It was not long into my sophomore year that Wendy and I broke up. I was left without my girlfriend and without my best friend. It was a perfect example of how I would constantly take and rarely give in my personal relationships.

I now take the opposite approach and constantly ask myself, *How can I add value to the lives of others?* By taking myself out of the equation and focusing on the needs of other people, I am able to selflessly add value to their lives and as a result, my life is much more fulfilling.

3

Yo Pal Hal Is Born

"Life experiences are like quarters—you lose both when you're sitting around on the couch."

—Jamba Juice® Cup

Though Jake's and my friendship had crumbled, my dream of becoming a professional disc jockey was launched. After enough persistence, I convinced my dad that I could make some real money doing the DJ thing. While on a trip to LA to visit my Aunt Belinda and Uncle Pete, I talked my dad into taking me by *Pro Sound & Stage Lighting*, a musical equipment store that produced my favorite mail-order catalogs. Walking onto the showroom floor, I felt like a big kid in a toy store, and the catalog that I had spent so many hours drooling over had come alive! There were giant speakers stacked throughout the room, laser lights hung from the roof, and bursts of fog shot past our feet and drifted up towards the ceiling, revealing the colorful beams of light that danced to the booms of the subwoofers.

My dad, who is also like a big kid in many ways, quickly grew as excited, if not more, than I was. After an hour or so of comparing products and negotiating prices, he ended up financing over $1,500 worth of equipment for me, with the agreement that I would be responsible for making the monthly payments. Though I did not realize it at the time, the reason I was successful in persuading Dad to help me get what I wanted was because I transferred my enthusiasm to him. That is exactly what sales is, a transfer of enthusiasm from one person to another about a product or service. Ever since you and I were children, we've been harmlessly and often unconsciously transferring our enthusiasm, or *selling* people, in order to help us get what we want.

Though I was excited and ready to start immediately, it was over a month before I was able to get my first real gig, and it happened by chance—me being in the right place at the right time. Dad and I were at the grocery store and he was ringing up a customer while I bagged her groceries. She enthusiastically shared the news that she was getting married and had so much to do in preparation of the event. She then mentioned how she had to get either a band or a DJ to play music for the reception.

Seizing the opportunity, Dad then told her how I was starting a DJ business and I had all the necessary equipment. She turned to me and asked me how much I charged. Her question caught me by surprise. At the time I had no idea what the going rate was, and when I timidly suggested a fee of $100, her jaw almost dropped to the ground.

For a fleeting moment I thought I was asking too much, but she eagerly agreed and hired me on the spot.

Eventually I became more in tune with the industry and set my fee at $75 per hour. From that moment though, my DJ business took off with weddings, school dances, private parties and even car shows. Come year's end, I had earned $5,600 for 80 hours of work. I was on my way!

Shortly after my business was in full swing, a woman who lived close by mentioned to my mom that they were looking for a high school student to be a DJ on the local radio station, 1090 AM. As any proud parent would, my mom mentioned that I was a DJ, and happy to hear the news, the woman suggested that I go down and apply for the job right away. Heeding her advice, I went to the station the next day.

The interview went fantastically well and I was hired that week. I was to be teamed up with a senior from my school named Martin DeHaven, whose air name was *DJ Marty D.*

The station manager said that he was looking for something that the kids could tune into after school, and we would be signed up for the 3:00 to 7:00 time slot every Thursday. Martin and I agreed that our show would be called the *Boomin' System* with *DJ Marty D* and whatever air name I could come up with.

The next day, I was in the car with Mom driving to get something to eat when I told her I had no idea what my DJ name should be and the show was less than a week away. I was starting to get a bit nervous because of it, too.

She looked at me and said I should make it something catchy that rhymed with my name, like *Your Pal Hal,* or give it some funky undertone such as *Yo' Pal Hal.* I rolled my eyes and told her it sounded dorky and just started laughing at her idea of funky and hip. However, the day of my first show soon came around and I still hadn't thought of anything. Just prior to going on, I actually mentioned *Yo Pal Hal* to the station manager and he said it sounded cool and that I should use it. Considering that he was my mom's age I hesitated, but decided to go with *Yo Pal Hal* and have been using it as my moniker ever since.

The station was a classic country station that would usually play people such as Hank Williams, Johnny Cash, and Patsy Cline. However, the station-manager wanted us to do something different and gave us full authority on our show, so we played hip-hop and top 40. It was a big change from the station's standard programming. We took calls and played requests, gave away concert tickets, and even came up with a *Disco Funky Flashback* where I borrowed a few *Sounds of the 70's* albums from my dad and played classic disco hits such as the Bee Gees' *Stayin' Alive* and KC & the Sunshine Band's *Get Down Tonight*.

I was nervous on the first day of the show. My drive to the station that day was exciting, as I could not wait to be live *on air* for my first time. Once arriving, I met up with Martin Dehaven—*"DJ Marty D"*—and we went over our game plan. Martin was a big help, and by the end of the show, we were in good form.

We had the best time putting on our radio show and did so every Thursday afternoon for the entire school year. In my spare time, I would sit at home cutting out pictures and buzz words from magazines, organizing them into various *Boomin' System* collages, and then pinning them up all over town and the Yosemite High campus. It was an absolute blast for me.

Though DJing did not become my life-long career, it was extremely valuable for me. It was DJing that gave birth to my entrepreneurial spirit and taught me how to deal with my anxieties and insecurities. I also found that I could put my fears behind a more public and outgoing persona such as *Yo Pal Hal*. The experience is one I am truly thankful for and just goes to show that although your dreams can change, make the most of where you are because it will determine where you end up.

One thing I can promise you is that time will pass. Day will become night, and the sunrise will bring with it a new tomorrow. This is the rhythm of life. What you are doing with these precious moments today is creating your tomorrow. To paraphrase something a friend once told me, *"How you spend your days is the greatest measure of who you are becoming."* My question to you is: *Who are you becoming...?*

4

THE VECTOR OPPORTUNITY

"It is in our moments of decision that our destiny is shaped."

—Anthony Robbins

It was a no-brainer for me to attend college upon graduation, and I did, one and a half hour south of Oakhurst, at *College of the Sequoias* in Visalia. I really wanted to diversify my education and did not center my coursework on any future career plans. Instead, I was more focused on learning and improving myself. I placed importance on my education, but not so much on a specific degree or the resulting documentation.

At 19, I wrapped up my first two semesters at *College of the Sequoias* and began working at a major radio station, pursuing my dream of becoming a syndicated radio disc jockey. After endless badgering by my college friend, Teddy Watson, I agreed to put my dream on hold for a day and meet with Jesse Levine, the Fresno District Manager of Cutco Cutlery, and see what they had to offer. I agreed, mainly to get Teddy off my back, and although I didn't think it was for me, I was genuinely intrigued by the fact that Teddy actually made a living selling knives.

Teddy and I walked casually into the Fresno District Office of Vector Marketing, the distributor for Cutco Cutlery. We sauntered into a large training room complete with six evenly spread eight-foot brown tables and a large VECTOR banner displayed on the back wall. Within a few moments, Jesse walked into the room, and right away I could sense a positive presence about him. Standing about 6'3" with short, sandy blond hair and dressed in a grey business suit, he carried himself with confidence and certainty.

He greeted us immediately and wore a big grin. "What's up Teddy?" He extended his hand to shake Teddy's and then pulled him in for a hug.

The two guys were obviously good friends. Any observer could tell that, even if they had not known that Teddy had lived with Jesse and been his assistant manager the previous summer.

"Not much, Jess," Teddy replied. "I want you to meet my friend, Hal. I've been trying to convince him that he needs to sell knives with us. I'm telling you, Hal would do great!" Teddy continued, "I'm going to get some order forms and supplies, so tell my man, Yo Pal Hal, about sellin' blades."

Jesse had a kind smile and it put me at ease. There was something very charismatic about his personality, and I had a feeling I could learn a lot from him. I dove right in, asking him if the "knife-thing" was legitimate, and he assured me that it was. He then quoted a few statistics and testimonials, which further validated what Teddy had been saying all along. To my knowledge, there were many suspect selling opportunities out there, so I wanted to make sure Cutco was the real deal and not a pyramid scheme.

Jesse offered an in-depth explanation of the business and did a thorough job of answering my questions. He also introduced me to another rep in the office, Jeremy Katen, who I had a good feeling about and who seemed to be genuinely nice.

Before long, I was asking Jesse what I needed to do to start selling Cutco. The idea fascinated me, and from the family feeling I got in the office, I knew I wanted to be a part of the team. Seeing my enthusiasm, Jesse told me that he could schedule me for the three-day training seminar starting the next day.

As much as I wanted to attend the seminar, the timing was not perfect. I explained that I could not start the next day because I had a new DJ job on 97.1 FM, and as the new guy I had to work the midnight to 6:00 a.m. shift. My objections did not faze Jesse and he confidently assured me that we could make it work. His being more confident that I should attend the training seminar than I was in saying I could not actually made the situation seem reasonable. Jesse closed the deal within minutes and it seemed the only logical choice was to forfeit my precious sleep and to DJ through the night while attending Cutco training all day. I am still amazed that Jesse was able to persuade me to commit to the training, which lasted six hours each day, Friday, Saturday and Sunday, but he did, and for that I am forever grateful.

I began training the next day, June 23, 1998, about a year and a half before the crash. Not really sure what to expect, I got a late jump on traffic and was running late to training. At the time, I was not even sure if I would keep the job. The whole idea of selling knives seemed strange to me. The positive feeling from the day before had worn off, and I worried that maybe Teddy and Jesse were just trying to pull me into a scam.

Training started at 9:00 a.m. on Friday, but I pulled into the Fresno Cutco office parking lot at 9:15 a.m.—15 minutes late. I did not have a good reason for my tardiness, but I quickly thought up a far-fetched story, hoping it would get Jesse laughing. I felt my cheeks turn red as I entered the crowded training room of about 25 people. I was dressed in my amateur business attire: Khakis, my dad's oversized dress shirt, and one of his maroon ties. Jesse was in the front of the room introducing himself, and discussing the training agenda for the next two days. He stopped and turned to see who had just entered and his eyes quickly locked on mine.

I began acting as if I was out of breath and desperately searching for air. I spoke fast and acted as shocked as I could. Then I began my glorious story.

"Sorry I'm late everybody. Jesse, you'll never guess what happened. So, I'm driving to training, on schedule to be about fifteen minutes early, when I see a car pulled over on the side of the freeway. There was a woman in the back seat and her legs were hanging out of the car. She looked in trouble, so I pulled over behind her and slowly approached the vehicle to find the woman in labor. I've never performed labor before, but what I am going to do, right? I knew what had to be done. To make a long story short—I delivered the baby, right there on the freeway! They were both okay when the paramedics showed up, and she was so grateful that she is going to name the baby *Hal!*"

Everyone looked at me strangely as if I had lost my mind. Jesse knew I was joking, yet I could tell by his smile that he appreciated the effort and may have been even a little impressed by my story.

"All right Hal, go ahead and grab a seat," he said still wearing his big grin. I did as instructed and Jesse continued with training completely undistracted by my interruption. Then Jesse introduced his partner in the office, V. John Baker. V. John was an experienced ex-Cutco District Manager, who had just recently moved to Fresno to help Jesse and the Fresno team become the first Vector office to reach $1,000,000 in sales. V. John was a very creative and innovative character, and wound up having a tremendous impact on me in my early Cutco career.

Jesse continued by telling his personal story of joining Cutco and what the experience had meant to him. He relayed that all of his friends thought he was crazy for selling knives. They constantly teased him and called him witty names such as *knife nerd* and *Ginsu boy.* He further explained how nervous and skeptical he had been during his training and first few weeks with Cutco. His family was unsupportive and made him question the idea of selling knives. He also said that he did not feel competent and confident in his ability to sell.

The training room was completely silent. In just a few

sentences, Jesse had managed to connect with everyone in the room. Every person sitting there had felt at least one, if not all, of the emotions and thoughts that Jesse had just described to us.

The tone of his voice was comforting, relating how any time anyone starts something new, you're bound to feel nervous and inadequate, but that passes with time and experience. "You can do this, and you are going to do great," he said smiling a thoughtful and sincere smile.

Now that he had everyone's complete attention, he began discussing Cutco's 50-year history. While this would seem like an appropriate time for me to catch up on the sleep that I had lost the night before, I doubt that anyone in the room even blinked.

As training concluded that day, I left with a lot of excitement about Cutco products and the opportunities that were available to me. After I spoke to a few other people, it became clear that their fears had been replaced with a bit of self-assurance, and they, too, were eager to start doing Cutco demos.

I called my mother as soon as I got onto the road. I relayed to her as much as I could recall about training, and she asked me if I was *still sure about this*. I could hear the doubt in her voice, but I exclaimed that I was more certain than ever and even insisted that she was going to love Cutco.

My night at the station flew by swiftly, and every spare moment in thought was spent reveling in the possibilities of success I could have with Vector. After six hours on the air at Q97, I drove back to my second day of training on time, but significantly sleepier than the day before. Nonetheless, I was excited to be there and ready to learn more about selling Cutco.

Jesse started the day teasing us about a Fast-Start Contest, building our interest. Then he broke us into groups again and asked us to continue role-playing the presentation. We used our knives from home to compare the Cutco knives against, and Jesse showed us how to cut pennies with the Cutco Super Shears.

Throughout the morning, Jesse probed the room and offered his expertise freely, never in a negative way, but rather in an encouraging way. Although it was not obvious to me at the time, every time I role-played, I was gaining confidence in myself and in the presentation.

Finally, Jesse approached the front of the room and without saying a word, wrote on the white board in large capitals, FAST-START CONTEST. He had done such a fantastic job building the anticipation during the last two days that by now, every one of us was eager to know what it was.

Cutco prizes were offered as incentives. Prizes increased in value depending on how much we sold, with levels from $1,000-$10,000. If any of us were to break the all-time Western Zone Fast-Start record of $12,733, we would take home every prize on the list as well as win an all expenses paid night-on-the-town in San Francisco, which included a free limo ride and dinner at a five-star hotel.

Then Jesse went into detail about the Fast-Start Contest record holders. The national record was set seven years prior by

Ong Mok Shin. He was a Korean immigrant who barely spoke English, knew almost no one in America, but he believed in the product and outworked everyone else.

Jesse shared that he was at the conference, years ago, when Ong Mok Shin accepted his award. Jesse relayed Ong Mok Shin's acceptance speech. He said, *"When you eat, I work. When you sleep, I work. When you work, I work harder!"* We chuckled at Jesse's impression, but the reality of it was that Ong Mok Shin's story impressed me, and I took note of his hard work.

The new Western Zone record of $12,733 was set just one week before I started, by a girl who lived just one hour south of Fresno, in Bakersfield. Although I considered Ong Mok Shin's $23,000 to be out of reach, I felt a rush of confidence come over me when I learned that the girl who just broke the Zone record lived only an hour south of us. I thought *if she could do it, why not me?*

By the time Jesse had gone over all of the details, the room was sitting on needles. When he finally closed the seminar for the day, everyone cheered, gathered their things quickly and bolted, but not before getting their seemingly mandatory high-five from Jesse. I remember thinking, "Geez, what's with this guy and his *high-fiving* everybody all the time?" Regardless, everyone was obviously excited, and I'm sure equally nervous to get home and start making calls to set up their initial practice appointments.

I lingered awhile, waiting to talk to Jesse, and feeling a burning desire that I had never felt before. Throughout my entire life, I had always been average. I maintained mediocre grades at best, was never an exceptional athlete, and when it came to popularity at school, I was easily overlooked. In other words, I had never really been a *star* at anything. But something about my new job inspired me. So, I approached Jesse and blurted out that I wanted to break the Fast-Start record. I was overwhelmed with excitement, yet Jesse remained calm. He looked at me, smiled, and said that he had heard this many times before. He said that a lot of people get excited in training, but no one has ever been willing to commit to the effort that it would take to break the record.

Before reason had its chance to set in, I spoke straight from my heart. "Jesse, I will sell more than $12,733 and break the Fast-Start record... just tell me what I have to do," I stated with a sort of blind conviction.

Jesse tested my resolve by continuing to tell me how difficult a task this was. He said that he could tell me how to do it, but only if I was willing to commit to the effort. I said that I was and I meant it. Nervous and scared, I decided to go for it. For the first time in my life, I was going to do something extraordinary. I thanked Jesse for his support and he said that I'd better get home and start calling people right away. He reminded me to call him as soon as I set my first appointment, so that we could celebrate.

I drove straight home, pulled my script from my training manual, and practiced it a few times. Once I had it down, I began calling through my list of people, mostly family that lived close by in Oakhurst, friends of my parents, and the parents of my friends from school. After setting my first appointment, I called Jesse and he said to set three more and call him back. By the end of the night, I managed to exceed the goal Jesse had set for me and scheduled a total of 16 appointments, two of which were set for after my third day of training.

I couldn't wait to tell Jesse the news, so I called him right away. At the time, he happened to be at the office with V. John and they were both equally excited. I could tell that they were sincerely invested in my success. They told me I was *awesome*, wished me well on my radio show, and said to keep up the amazing work. Their belief in me was all I needed to keep myself going.

I left Oakhurst that night at around 10:00 p.m. to make it on time to my shift at the radio station by midnight. I was jazzed from my Cutco training and the possibilities that were ahead, and it definitely came across in my enthusiasm on the air. Oddly enough, my dream job of DJing on the radio was the last thing on my mind, and I just couldn't wait to sell Cutco.

Before signing off at 6:00 a.m., I had an idea to do something special; I popped a blank tape into the recorder and turned on my microphone, "All right Q97 listeners, my time is up and Danny P will be playing today's hit music for you through the morning. But before I go, I want to give a shout-out to Jesse Levine, V. John Baker, and my entire Cutco crew. Stay positive and keep slingin' those blades! This is Yo Pal Hal signing off."

I showed up Sunday for my third day of training very proud of my progress thus far and ready to conquer the world, or at least the Fast-Start record. I caught up with Jesse just before training and asked if I could play a special tape for our group. He seemed to trust me, and I played the recording of my sign-off earlier that morning. Jesse approved and smiling said, "Yo Pal Hal, huh...? I like it!"

I could barely contain myself all day long, eagerly awaiting my opportunity to get to my first appointment. When training was done, Jesse released us into the real world and said that we could only achieve what we thought our best was. I knew my best was soon to come and felt armed and prepared with the tools I needed to meet my goals.

Determined to break the Fast-Start record and feeling confident in my newfound ability to sell Cutco, I promised Jesse and V. John that I was going to sell my first Homemaker +8 set that night, and that I was on a mission to sell over $1,000 for the day. Jesse offered me a few encouraging words and sent me out to conquer my first two appointments, but not before giving me a now welcomed *high-five*. What can I say; the whole *positive thinking* thing was growing on me.

I walked out of the Fresno Cutco office that day having

made a *decision*—to break the Fast-Start record—but I had no way of knowing that this decision was going to shape the rest of my life.

5

GETTING OFF TO A FAST-START

"There is always a way... if you're committed."

—Romacio Fulcher

I sped out of the parking lot eager to get to my first demo. Jesse had advised me to set my first few appointments with people I thought would be most likely to purchase Cutco, so that I could gain confidence and experience success right away. I had scheduled my first demo for the evening with my Nana and Papaw, and my second demo with their neighbors, Jack and Delores Allison. These were family and friends whom I thought would surely buy a set of Cutco from me—even if they did so just to help me out.

I arrived a few minutes early, said hello to my grandparents, and then dove into my presentation. I was a bit unorganized and fumbling through my words, as well as my Cutco samples, and I was completely unprepared for their objections. In training I learned what to say if they said *it was too much money* or *they wanted to think about it*, but my grandparents objected that they were *too old* to buy new knives. I didn't know how to respond, and feeling helpless, I found myself losing my cool and arguing the value of Cutco with them. This was a reflection of my immaturity and lack of experience. I would later learn that arguing with a customer never works.

So, Nana and Papaw didn't buy anything, and I was pretty taken aback by my first *no sale*. But I was determined to do better on my next presentation. With my sample kit under my arm, I walked next door to Jack and Delores' house, and this time I delivered my presentation flawlessly, only to hear the same objection—they were too old to buy knives.

My confidence was crushed. My level-ten enthusiasm that I had sustained for the past three days had plummeted to about a level two. If I could not sell these fantastic knives to my own grandparents and their life-long neighbors, how would I ever succeed with average customers? I felt hopeless and lost confidence that I could make a single sale, let alone beat the Fast-Start record.

Embarrassed and defeated, I reluctantly called Jesse. As I expected, he was excited to hear how I had done. When I told him I had failed and sold nothing, I thought that his enthusiasm would drop as well. I thought wrong.

Instead, Jesse was calm and reassuring. He told me that this was normal, and that it was no big deal. He reminded me about the *Law of Averages* he had taught us in training. Some people buy and some people don't, but it always averages out. He said there were two ways in which I could respond to my first day of no-sales. "Hal, most people would probably be discouraged and give up going for the Fast-Start record at this point. They would quit before they had really even given themselves a chance to succeed."

I interrupted, "Yeah, go on, that's pretty much how I'm feeling."

"But Hal, I don't think you are like most people. In fact, I know you're not." Then Jesse explained his *Five-minute Rule— it's okay to be negative, but not for more than five minutes.* He said that I could get angry, upset, and emotional about what had happened, but for only five minutes; then I had to figure out a solution. I gained nothing by wasting any more time worrying, but I gained everything by putting it behind me and moving forward.

He was quiet for a moment, and I let his words sink in. Then he added, "Here's what I think you should do. Go home, get on the phone, and make more calls than you were planning on making. Go out tomorrow, do eight appointments and have a grand day!"

In Cutco terms, a *grand day* is when you sell $1,000 or more in a single day, an accomplishment I desperately wanted, as it would be the first step I would need to take if I was to make up ground and reach my goal. With every encouraging word Jesse spoke, I could feel the weight of disappointment and fear lifting off me. Inspired by Jesse's confidence in me, I felt determined and positive once again.

Despite being filled earlier with fear and self-doubt, I went home and made the phone calls. I surprised even myself and scheduled another 10 appointments, determined not to let this small bump in the road interfere with my journey to success. My mind was racing that evening as I lay down to bed, filled with conflicting emotions of fear and excitement. It had been so easy to maintain my confidence in training, but it was so much more difficult to be self-assured in the face of defeat. I had no idea what the next nine days would bring, but I committed to Jesse that I would put forth the effort, and I wasn't about to let him down.

I woke up ready to sell again. I left my house for my first full day as a Cutco rookie, and worked from 7:00 a.m. until 10:30 p.m. I completed 10 demos and sold on seven of the 10, making my total sales for the day $2,768. I earned my first increase in commission, and succeeded beyond my wildest expectations.

I could not believe it! I went home that night completely astonished by my feat, not to mention how much money I had made. My head was reeling with the numbers. The second I walked in the door, I ran for the calculator and quickly calculated my commission. After my first full day of work, I made almost $400. Not only had I achieved my first promotion, I was only $232 away from my second promotion. I could barely contain my excitement, so after I danced about the house with my mom, singing Cutco's praises, I called Jesse. He was proud and equally happy for me. He told me to take my excitement and put it to good use. I loved how Jesse would gladly celebrate with me, but then immediately get me focused on *what's next*.

I took his advice quite literally and got up early the next

morning to make more phone calls. I worked all day doing demos and finished up the evening with phone time at 9:00 p.m. It was non-stop and I loved every minute of it. I was on a constant adrenaline rush. I talked to Jesse and V. John about 20 times a day, getting support after challenging demos and celebrating my success with them when I made sales.

By day three of the Fast-Start Contest, my parents had joined my team and were on board with my mission of breaking the Fast-Start record. They abandoned their skepticism and became my greatest supporters. In fact, if they saw me sitting around they would ask, "Shouldn't you be making phone calls?" It was such a supportive atmosphere. My parents not only loved the changes they were seeing in me, but my positive energy and attitude was actually changing them, too.

During the Fast-Start Contest, I was still working on Fridays and Saturdays as a DJ for Q97. The two weekends during the Fast-Start played out like this. I woke up Friday morning around 7:00 a.m. to make phone calls and did demos all day until around 9:00 p.m. Then I jumped into my red GMC Sonoma pickup and drove an hour and a half to Visalia, where I was on the air from 12:00 a.m. – 6:00 a.m. After my shift, I drove home early Saturday morning, took a shower and started the entire cycle over again. I didn't sleep and I took no breaks for naps or coffee. After I had finished the weekend and booked my final appointments on Sunday night, I was absolutely exhausted, yet exhilarated at the same time.

To this day, I am still amazed at the transformation that took place in me. All I know is that I saw a phenomenal opportunity in Cutco, I got excited, and I went for it. I was fueled by the sheer drive and desire to achieve my goal. I quit my so-called dream job at the radio station after working only two weekends with Cutco. Cutco was truly an unexpected dream come true.

I woke the last day of my Fast-Start Contest with a heavy weight on my shoulders. It was the final day to achieve my goal, and although I had managed to sell $10,928 in my first nine days, I still needed $1,806 to break the record.

I did not let my nervousness or fear of failure stop me. Any time those negative *what if* thoughts came into my head, I would just push them out and proclaim to the heavens, "I am going to break the Fast-Start record!"

Once I made that decision, everything seemed easier. I was motivated by my desire to succeed at a level that I had never known. And succeed I did. I had six appointments set that last day, and made six sales, totaling $4,130 CPO. My final appointment of the day was with Harry Baker, President and owner of Sierra Telephone, my mom's former employer. Harry, known for his generosity, bought the biggest order of my Fast-Start, over $1,400 worth of the World's Finest Cutlery!

Not only did I break the Western Zone Fast-Start record, but I raised the bar significantly higher so that future Cutco sales representatives would have something to strive for, by setting the new Zone Fast-Start record at $15,058.

On that day, a new Hal Elrod was born. Although I may not have seen it while it was happening, my Fast-Start experience was more about who I was becoming through the process than it was about any money or recognition. The old Hal would never imagine such a thing; the new Hal could see it no other way. The day I broke the record, because of who I had become during those 10 days, represents my best day ever.

When all was said and done, I completed 62 demos during the Fast-Start Contest, and I made 42 sales. That means that 20 people told me "no," rejected and refused to buy from me. I learned from the experience that rejection is part of life. It is not inherently good or bad, it just is what it is. However, because rejection is inevitable, we must learn to overcome it.

By the end of the Fast-Start contest I had matured a great deal and became a much more confident and able person. I became equipped with the emotional fortitude to endure and overcome future obstacles and rejections. I became the man who would be able to handle the biggest challenge life would throw my way.

In Cutco, it was not that I found myself, but by actualizing the potential that is within me—within all of us—I created a better version of myself. This process of personal growth is something that I have committed to continue for the rest of my life, always striving to be better. The Japanese call this philosophy *kaizen,* which means *constant and never-ending improvement in both personal and professional life.* Have you committed to continuously improving yourself? If you have not, now is a great time to consider making that commitment. After all, you have nothing to lose and everything to gain.

Inevitably, your personal and professional life will be plagued with difficulties and failures. However, this is not necessarily a bad thing. In fact, whether your difficulties and failures are good or bad is entirely up to you, for it is not what happens to us that matters, it is how we respond to what happens to us that determines our life.

I fail, you fail—everyone fails. So what separates successful people from failures? Successful people keep on trying, despite their fear of failing. Successful people do not label their failure as a *bad* thing. They see it as a necessary and unavoidable part of the process of success, and they learn from their failures.

My secret to success has been simple: despite my fears, inadequacies, self-doubt, and numerous obstacles... *I keep on trying. I continue to create consistent progress towards the life of my dreams.* The only failure would be in giving up. The road to success can be long, but if you keep on trying—never ceasing to *create consistent progress* in the direction of your goals and dreams—your success is inevitable. Guaranteed.

6

BECOMING A CHAMPION

"I've always believed that if you put in the work,
the results will come."

—Michael Jordan

My first ten days selling Cutco were filled with a myriad of challenges and victories, of disappointments and celebrations, all of which were new to me.   Directly after my Fast-Start concluded, I entered into my very first Push Period. This was a two-week long sales competition that preceded the Western Zone's Summer Conference One (SC1), and all reps that would be attending the conference were competing for the top spot.

Still on a frantic selling spree, I was working diligently every day and seldom taking any time off from Cutco, but I loved every minute. Although I did not realize it at the time, I was becoming an *achiever*, and my desire to achieve at higher and higher levels continued to grow with each accomplishment.

At first, I did not fully understand what Push Period was. Jesse and V. John kept hyping it up at our weekly Team Meetings and promoting it virtually every time I called into the office. Jesse would even wake me up in the morning with a phone call, screaming into the phone at the top of his lungs, "IT'S   PUUSSSSHHHH   PEEERRRRIIIIOOOODDDD!"

Needless to say, I was getting the impression that it was a pretty big deal.

Jesse used friendly competition to motivate me, pitting me against a sales rep from the Santa Rosa office by the name of Adam Curchack, the top Cutco rep in the Western Zone. According to Jesse and V. John, Adam thought that no one could beat him, but they assured me I would be the one to do it.

Fueled by the momentum I had created during my Fast-Start, I continued to work at a frantic pace. Although I was still somewhat insecure and unsure of my ability, I didn't allow myself much time to sit and think as I was constantly taking action and charging forward. Whenever I had bad days and began to doubt myself, Jesse was there to pick me up. I was learning the value of having a mentor, and without Jesse's support I would have given up on many occasions.

The details of my first Push Period are nearly identical to those of my Fast-Start; ups and downs; good days and bad days. I finished my last appointment of the Push Period and drove straight from Oakhurst down to the Cutco office in Fresno. My suitcase was packed for our three-day conference in San Francisco, and I walked into the Fresno office armed with a thick stack of orders. Thirty or so of my teammates were spread throughout the room, and I immediately spotted my partner from training. "Sam, what's up buddy? How have you been?"

He smiled, "Great, but not as good as you from what I've heard!"

"Yeah, it's been kinda crazy! How have your sales been?"

"Good, I'm really looking forward to the advanced sales training we are going to get at the conference. How much did you sell for Push Period?"

"Honestly, I don't even know. I know I'm over $10,000, but I'm not sure by how much." I spotted V. John sitting at his desk, sifting through orders with a calculator in hand. I plopped my stack in front of him and asked him if he would add them up for me and tell me my total.

Jesse appeared with Jeremy and smiled wide, "Dude, what's up Hal?"

I gave them both an enthusiastic high-five. "Not much Jesse, I'm just fired-up for the conference!" I had added all sorts of new words and phrases into my vocabulary after starting with Cutco—*awesome, fired-up, poz*(positive)—and I loved the uplifting verbiage.

"Yeah, it's going to be awesome. Hey, do you want to ride up there with me, Jeremy, and V. John?"

"Heck yeah!" I quickly agreed, and Jeremy and I secured our spots in the backseat of Jesse's Honda Accord. The rest of the Fresno team piled into their cars and we all caravanned to San Francisco. V. John added up my orders in the car and told me what my total was, but he stressed to keep it a secret until the Push Period count-up. Apparently that was part of the fun, how no one knew how much anyone else had sold until the moment of truth.

When we arrived at the hotel, Jeremy and I found our way straight to our destination, which was just as Jesse and V. John had described. The conference room was immense, and crowds of reps were piling in the double doors to take their seats. Upbeat techno music pumped through the sound system and I could feel the energy. On the walls hung huge banners displaying logos such as *Fired-Up Knife Selling Machine* and *Summer Excellence Awards,* as well as others recognizing the eight Divisions in attendance. I quickly spotted the *Nor Cal Division* banner and felt a sense of pride come over me.

Long rows of folding metal chairs stretched from one side of the room to the other. Up front was a stage, framed by two long tables displaying what could only be the coveted push period trophies that Jesse had so enthusiastically promoted.

Jeremy and I grabbed seats up front and blocked off a section for our Fresno team. Suddenly I felt a tap on my shoulder. I turned around to find V. John accompanied by a young man who looked a few years older than me; he had reddish hair and wore a shirt and tie, much like the one I borrowed that morning from my dad.

"Hal, I want you to meet somebody," V. John said. "This is Adam Curchack, from the Santa Rosa office. He's the number-one rep in the Western Zone for the year, and I think you guys should get to know each other since you are competing this summer. I'll leave you to get acquainted."

Adam seemed a little on-edge. "Hal, dude, V. John told me

you sold something like $15,000 for your Fast-Start and that you had a pretty big Push Period," he said with a laid-back tone and demeanor. He continued, "So, how much did you sell for Push Period?"

"Umm, uh, I thought we weren't supposed to tell anyone how much we sold until the count-up," I replied, not too sure of myself.

"Dude, it's just a Push Period; it's not even a big deal. You can tell me how much you sold."

Feeling a little bit intimidated, I decided to stand my ground. "No, that's okay. I'll just wait until the count-up."

"Whatever dude, I'll see you on stage." Adam turned and walked over to talk to a group of sales reps. I returned to my seat, unable to recognize anyone except for my fellow Fresno teammates.

The music faded out. Everyone began to take their seats as a good-looking man in a dark blue suit approached the podium. Speaking firmly into the microphone he began, "Hello everyone! My name is Bruce Goodman; I'm your Zone Manager, and I'd like to welcome you to the 1998 Western Zone Summer Conference One. I am truly honored to be the host of this weekend's event, and I want to congratulate each of you for being here today."

Mr. Goodman went on to explain what we could expect to gain from the conference over the next three days. After 30 minutes of introductions and announcements, Bruce Goodman stood by himself behind the podium and took a deep breath. He wore a satisfied grin on his face, and we all sat at attention awaiting his next words. "So, I hear you guys sold some knives these last two weeks, is that right?"

The crowd answered with enthusiastic hoots and hollers, assuring him that indeed some knives had been sold!

"All right, that's what I like to hear. I know that everyone has been working exceptionally hard the last couple of weeks, and we'd like to recognize you for your efforts. I have 20 Push Period trophies up here to be awarded to the top 20 sales leaders, but only one #1 trophy for our overall winner. So, please make your way to the front of the room and let's begin the Summer Conference One Push Period count-up!"

This was it, the moment of truth. Reps made their way to the front of the room and lined up behind two microphones, one on either side of the stage. One by one, they stepped forward to announce their sales reports into the microphones. I sat anxiously in the back, and watched the count-up unfold. Bruce continued to announce each consecutive sales level:

$1,500 to $2,000...

$2,000 to $2,500...

$2,500 to $3,000...

Each new level brought forth another group of sales reps to the microphone. And at each level, the crowd on either side of the stage was thinning as people gave their sales report and returned to their seats. As the number of reps who remained standing shrunk smaller, my nervousness only escalated.

Occasionally, I would glance across the stage to check if Adam Curchack was still standing, and each time I did, he was. He appeared relaxed and it was obvious this wasn't his first Push Period. While I was standing on needles and selfishly praying for my own victory, he was casually leaning against the stage with a self-assured smirk that said, "I can't be beat." Who was I to disagree?

It took some time, but finally we got down to the top 20, all over 5,000 in sales, and Bruce Goodman invited us to join him on stage. Making my way onto the platform, I spotted Jesse sitting in the front row amongst my Fresno team. Our eyes met, and he nodded in approval as I smiled back nervously. The bright stage lights made me squint my eyes. Even so, as I stood above the audience, I gained a new perspective to the massive number of people in attendance. Looking from side to side, and not recognizing anyone, I felt like the new kid on my first day of school.

Bruce stepped aside allowing us to give our sales reports at the podium and continued with the count-up. It moved quickly now. Half of the group stepped forward between $5,000 and $7,000 dollars, and seven of the final ten went down before Bruce reached the $9,500 mark. Each sales report given at the microphone prompted cheers from the crowd, and now only three of us were left. Adam and I remained on stage with one other rep; some kid named Jesus, who wore a grey suit and appeared to be my age. Bruce had the floor.

"Wow, what a great job everyone has done. We have three trophies left, and we are fast approaching a magical number in Vector Marketing. Ten-thousand-dollars sold during a Push Period represents the highest level reached by our top achievers. In fact, it was only a few years ago that Jesse Levine, now our District Manager in Fresno, became the first rep in the Western Zone ever to sell $10,000 for a Push Period. Today, it looks as though we may have three. Okay, is anyone between $9,500 and $10,000...?" You could hear a pin drop in the room as the crowd looked on in silence.

I swallowed hard as Jesus, myself, and Adam all stood tall, not a single one of us stepping forward.

"Are you all over TEN... THOUSAND... DOLLARS...?"

We nodded simultaneously to confirm that we indeed were. Bruce made an official announcement into the microphone, and the crowd cheered in approval. The way I felt was beyond description. For the first time in my life, I was standing on top of a stage, but it felt as if I were standing on top of the world. Never had I experienced such an emotional high, but the count-up was not over yet.

Just squeaking over with $10,000 and change, Jesus accepted the third place trophy and took it with his newfound glory back to his seat. His team welcomed him with congratulations and high-fives. Bruce turned his attention back to Adam and me. By now, both of us were as nervous as two boys on our first dates, and each could only blindly guess what the other had sold. Standing there with no experience and nowhere to pull confidence from, I feared the unknown and thought for sure that Adam was going to beat me.

"Well, we have our veteran Field Sales Manager, Adam Curchack from the Santa Rosa office, who is no stranger to Push Periods. And it is my pleasure to introduce our new Fast-Start record breaker, Hal Elrod, from the Fresno office. Everyone, Hal just finished up his Fast-Start a couple of weeks ago and in case you didn't hear, he sold $15,058 in his first 10 days! I think that deserves a round of applause.

All right, let's see which one of you finished up on top. Now that we're down to our top two reps, I'm going to continue in increments of $100. Did either of you sell between $10,100 and $10,200...?

Neither of us budged.

$10.200 to $10,300...?

$10,300 to $10,400...?"

With each hundred-dollar increment, I silently prayed Adam would step forward.

"$10,400 to $10,500...?"

Bruce continued to count higher as the tension mounted, but neither one of us moved.

"Are you both over ELEVEN... THOUSAND... DOLLARS?"

Yes, dammit, BOTH of us!

Bruce continued his seemingly endless count… although, when he reached $11,600, something unbelievable occurred; Adam took a step forward.

Did this mean what I thought it meant?

Jesse jumped up from his chair and screamed, "Yeeeaahhh!" The entire Fresno team followed his lead, leaping to their feet and cheering for me. My heart skipped a beat. The background melted and the scene became surreal.

Adam grabbed the microphone from Bruce's hand and muttered the sweetest words I had ever heard, "I'm Adam Curchack from the Santa Rosa Alliance, and I sold $11,611 for the Push Period." Bruce shook Adam's hand and awarded him the #2 trophy. Adam turned to me and offered his hand, which I shook enthusiastically. Then he walked off the stage, leaving only Bruce and me, standing taller than ever.

"We have our winner. Congratulations Hal, let's find out how high you finished up. Where were we?

$11,700 to $11,800…?

$11,800 to $11,900…?

$11,900 to $12,000…?"

Bruce continued to count higher and higher, with each thousand dollars bringing a round of applause from the audience.

When Bruce reached $15,000 Jesse brought a chair up on stage for me to sit in, playfully suggesting that I was going to be up there for awhile. Although it was humorous, I did not want to seem arrogant, so I politely declined. Everyone watched in awe as Bruce and I played this game of mystery that Vector called a count-up for a while longer.

When I finally stepped forward—at just over $18,000—the crowd exploded in ovation. An audience of nearly one thousand Cutco representatives stood applauding, whistling, and cheering. Jesse was going nuts and every one of my Fresno teammates was on their feet. This seemed to go on forever, and I actually had to wait for the room to quiet down before I could announce my total. I was glad to wait. I had gone from standing on top of the world to now hovering somewhere in outer space.

Accepting the microphone from Mr. Goodman, I inhaled deeply and struggled to remember the Fresno Empire chant. "Hello, my name is Hal Elrod from the Fresno—"

"EMPIRE!" my team shouted back.

"And I'm striking back with a C3PO of $18,036 for Push Period."

The crowd cheered as I pumped my fist in exhilaration. All the hard work did pay off, and now I finally had the opportunity to sit back and enjoy the moment.

Looking around the large room, I took notice of my new group of Cutco friends who would soon become like my family. Though we all were competing for our own personal glory, the bottom line was that we were all one group, one team, and everybody on their feet cheering was a prime example of that. My Push Period record was a victory for the entire company. It was the result of the world's finest product, an incredible support staff, a lot of hard work on my part, God's blessings, and a bit of luck. I was humbled by the cheers and honored to be a member of the team.

The next three days felt like I was in a movie—*not like my real life.* The conference was very informative and I learned a lot of great selling tips, but I'm referring to my first taste of being a *Vector celebrity.* Everyone wanted to talk to me, and reps continuously approached me with pen and pad, practically begging for me to tell them my *secrets* for selling Cutco!

What secrets were they referring to? I was still figuring the job out for myself, and when asked for advice, I just repeated what Jesse had told us in training: *Just cut rope and smile!* I stayed up in the lobby every night at the conference, until at least 2:00 in the morning, teaching people my so-called secrets.

I even gave my first speech that weekend. It wasn't an organized message, in fact, it wasn't even written down. Bruce just asked me to share with everyone how I sold $18,036 for the Push. Although I was nervous before I went on stage to speak, once I was up there it came surprisingly naturally. I even had people cracking up when I told them about my favorite demo. It was one I'd done earlier that week, with some friends of my parents, Mark and Robyn. On the appointment they fed me tritip steak, gave me a rare Cutco carving knife from 1949 to show on my demos, bought $400 worth of Cutco, and even set me up on a date with their friend's beautiful daughter. And this was what Vector called work? What a blessing; I truly loved my job!

The conference really opened my eyes and I was fully committed to my success with Cutco. I went on to sell over $60,000 by the end of the year, which qualified me for the company trip to Cancun, Mexico. I began management training during the fall after I approached Jesse and told him that I wanted to help others to succeed, the way that he had helped me.

The following summer, at age 19, I moved to Sacramento and opened my very own Cutco Branch Office. This was a great opportunity for me to acquire an entirely new set of skills and forced me to grow up very quickly. I was responsible for saving $10,000 in start-up costs, finding an office space, setting it up with the necessary furniture and equipment, hiring a receptionist, placing advertisements in newspapers, handing out flyers at college campuses, running daily interviews, leading the same three-day training seminar that Jesse had led for me, and managing a team of 80 sales reps. It was the most difficult task I had ever taken on, and at the same time, the most rewarding. There was no better feeling for me than to coach my reps through their failures and celebrate their successes, the way Jesse had done with me.

I was very humbled by the challenge that came with managing my own team, as was my ego, when, during the first Summer Conference of 1999, my Push Period record was broken. I sat in the audience at the conference and watched the count-up unfold, as Jon Berghoff, an up-and-coming rep from the San Jose office, reported over $26,000 in sales! Although it hurt a bit to see my record go, I was genuinely impressed by such a feat, and excited for Jon to feel the same triumph that I had the summer before.

As a manager, I fared well but did not achieve the same level of record-breaking success that I had as a sales rep. I attribute this moderate performance to my overestimating my abilities and underestimating the challenge of managing an office.

At the end of the summer, I closed down my office and moved, with my new girlfriend, back to Fresno. A lot of changes were taking place; the Western Zone had been restructured and renamed the Western Region, giving my Division Manager, J. Brad Britton, a promotion to Regional Sales Director. Jesse also received a promotion, taking Brad's place as the Nor Cal Division Manager. This meant he would oversee about a dozen offices in our division, while continuing to run the Fresno office.

Jesse celebrated his new promotion by purchasing his first BMW—a goal he had set for himself back in high school—and I followed his example, buying my first new car—a white Ford Mustang.

Life was great, and living with a woman for the first time was helping me to grow in new ways. I was happy, I felt truly blessed, and I saw no limit to what was possible.

7

THAT NIGHT

"I claim not to have controlled events, but confess plainly that events have controlled me."

—Abraham Lincoln

Anxiety builds in my mind like a dense fog as the clock ticks away each opportune minute to leave this apartment on time. I can't concentrate. We are going to be late. My speech is not ready and my girlfriend will not stop yelling at me from the other room.

It is Friday afternoon, December 3, 1999, and I am standing in the dimly lit bathroom of our second-story apartment, focused intently on my reflection in the mirror. I find myself once again engaged in the recurring struggle to get a stubborn knot straight on an uncooperative tie, and it would appear that the tie is winning.

Although it's fighting me at the moment, this tie is my lucky one and has always seemed to work the fates in my favor. My favorite tie, sky-blue covered in navy-blue flowers, was given to me by my younger sister for my 20th birthday earlier in the year. Hayley has always possessed a keen fashion sense, and the tie she gave me is sure to put the finishing touches on my business attire, a white dress shirt fresh from the cleaners, tucked snuggly into my black pressed slacks, accented with a black leather belt and shiny black shoes.

I am itching to get on the road and for good reason. Parked underneath the carport in space #232 is every young man's dream: my brand new, bright white Ford Mustang that I drove home from the car lot three weeks ago. Owning a new car reminds me of having a new girlfriend; when I'm with her I'm euphoric and when we're apart, she's all I can think about. Although my baby is not the GT model with the V8 (those are too pricey and high-maintenance for me), she still pushes 190 horses under the hood, and with my five-speed transmission I control their every move. You might even say that with my shifter in hand, I am like Merlin with his wand, capable of creating magic at any moment.

Speaking of magic moments, I am hoping to create a few tonight when I deliver my speech to several dozen Cutco sales representatives in the Nor Cal Division of Vector Marketing and Cutco Cutlery. Most are college students. My message is titled 'Maximizing Push Period' and it's timed to build momentum for the Division Push Period that starts on Monday.

As usual, my nervousness is due to the fact that I am not as prepared as I should be. Instead, I will be reading from a page of poorly organized, unfinished notes and winging the rest of it. No matter how many times I give a speech, I still cannot seem to discipline myself to adequately prepare, but instead find myself procrastinating until the last possible moment. I find it interesting that my audience assumes I have it all together when nothing could be further from the truth.

Hastily fumbling through my assortment of keys, I lock up the apartment and scurry down the stairs to the car. We throw our stuff in the back seat of the Mustang and plop down onto the gray cloth seats as I stick the obnoxiously large black plastic Ford key into the ignition. The engine fires up and my tires screech as I speed out of the apartment complex toward northbound Highway 99. We have a 90-minute drive ahead of us until we get to the Modesto office, which is run by Anthony Pimentel, whom we call the *Big Dog* due to his NFL linebacker size.

At this point in time, my relationship with my girlfriend, Amber, is anything but idyllic. Living together is creating tension between us and as a result, typically our car rides find their way into an insignificant and usually pretty silly argument over something – or oftentimes nothing. Lately it's been over which one of our families we are going to spend the fast approaching holidays. In an attempt to avoid such an argument, I put in my newest *Dave Mathews Band* CD and keep it playing at a volume just loud enough to rule out the likelihood of conversation. Ironically Dave sings, *"So much to say, so much to say, so much to say, so much to saaayy..."*

Dave's sultry voice fades to background noise as my thoughts are consumed with tonight's speech. I have my mental pen and pad working diligently in my head, remembering what Jesse told me when I gave my first speech a year and a half ago. "Don't be nervous. Just make them laugh and have a good ending; you'll do great."

Good advice, but I have found that it is not that easy to be funny when you are trying to be and that it is difficult to come up with a good ending when you have no real beginning or middle.

As we cruise into Modesto, the sun is setting beyond the horizon and the sky bleeds a dark reddish-purple. The digital display on my Mustang's dash has a teal glow and reads 6:52. It is not long before we spot the green overhead freeway sign for our exit, and for a moment I feel relieved that we made it on time, but the feeling is quick to flee as a wave of nervousness for my speech rushes back.

We arrive at the large two-story office complex that is home to the Modesto Cutco Office. A handful of reps stand conversing outside and welcome us with a barrage of warm, enthusiastic greetings. "Hey, it's Hal and Amber! What's up guys?"

I quickly spot Anthony "Big Dog" Pimentel, Modesto's District Manager and the host of tonight's meeting, standing inside the doorway, holding a roll of red raffle tickets and sporting a red Santa hat. The theme of tonight's meeting is *Holiday Selling*, but being an ex-football player and an overall pretty big guy, I can't help but laugh at Big Dog's attire.

He extends his massive right hand to shake mine. "Mr. Hal Elrod, welcome to Mo-town; it's good to see you. And hello to you Amber; happy early birthday."

"Hello Anthony," Amber replies with a warm smile.

I feebly attempt to give Anthony my firmest handshake. "It's good to see you too Big Dog. Congratulations, by the way, I saw Modesto toward the top of the newsletter last week. You guys are doing awesome!"

"Thanks." Extending his right hand toward the front of the room he adds, "We're about to get started, why don't you and Amber go ahead and grab seats up front."

Tonight's meeting is scheduled to last from 7:00-9:00 p.m.; then our plan is to go out to eat at Buck's Steakhouse in celebration of Amber's upcoming birthday. Taking into consideration the one-and-a-half-hour drive back to Fresno, we should be home before midnight. As we take our seats, I immediately pull my speech from my bag and frantically continue to work on it. My thoughts are soon interrupted though by a familiar voice.

"Hello, can you hear me in the back?" Jesse's voice echoes out into the room.

I look up from my notebook to find my mentor, standing at the podium, adjusting the microphone. Jesse's broad shoulders fill out a classic gray pinstriped business suit; his medium-length blond hair is messed with gel and that big 'Jesse Levine' smile stretches wide across his face. I'm still in awe every time I hear Jesse speak, as he is somewhat of a legend in the Cutco business. Last year, at the ripe age of 23, he led the Fresno 'Empire' team to become the first office in the 50-year history of Cutco products to surpass $1,000,000 in annual sales.

"If everyone could go ahead and please grab a seat, we're going to get started in just a minute," he adds.

Twenty or so professionally dressed young men and women scramble throughout the room to secure their position on one of the many tan, padded metal folding-chairs. Most of us are college students and have given up our Friday night to learn how to get better at selling knives.

From the moment that we were hired at Vector, we have faced opposition from our friends and family, as well as ourselves. We took a chance on an opportunity that, in most cases, our circle of influence did not support. We've also been challenged by our own self-doubt, skepticism, and the bad habits that come with being an average teenager. Oftentimes, we are our own worst enemy in trying to succeed, and it is only with the support of others that we are able to make it through the tough times.

As for our parents, mine were skeptical from the start, but I was able to gain their support by working hard and creating almost immediate results for myself. Most young people who start selling Cutco aren't as fortunate, and have to fight an uphill battle with mom and dad from day one. As you can probably imagine, not too many kids go home after being hired by Vector and hear their parents say anything along the lines of, "Great work son, we always hoped you would someday sell knives in strangers' homes."

The Vector opportunity can change the life of any young person as it has done for me, but sadly, I have seen many reps quit prematurely because of their family's lack of support, before they have really given themselves the chance to succeed. Those who are here tonight have either gotten the support they needed from home, or taken action despite any opposition they've faced. We are here because we believe; we are excited for our futures, and I would say that most of us are serious about our success.

I look around and see most of the crowd in attendance all gazing intently on Jesse. I notice how calm and cool he is, and hope I can find the same strength when it is my turn to take the podium.

Why do I always do this? Why do I always wait until the last minute? It is no mystery; I know the answers to these questions. I procrastinate because I am afraid that the speech I write won't be perfect, and so rather than just doing the inevitable, I resist doing it until it's too late. Then I leave it up to chance and hope my personality is good enough to pull it off. No matter how my speech turns out, though, I always end up feeling disappointed in myself knowing that I didn't do my best.

My message, *Maximizing Push Period*, is intended to get this group excited for the Push Period that starts on Monday. For me, Push Periods have been a lot like the play-offs for Michael Jordan, giving me an opportunity to learn what it takes to be a champion. And like any champion, I have been humbled during my moments of defeat. I am amongst a few of my colleagues as well as some new talent, and who knows what the next two weeks of selling will bring. All I can do is put forth my best effort and work hard every day until the Division Meeting, and pray for the strength to do it.

Before taking the job with Vector, I considered myself a lazy person, and in many ways, I still do. Throughout the last year and a half I have been inconsistent with my sales from week-to-week and month-to-month. However, when a Push Period rolls around, I transform like the mild-mannered Bruce Banner into the fiercely intense Hulk. Driven by the challenge of competition, I make a commitment to work from sunrise to sunset for two weeks straight, because my experience has taught me that *on the day of victory, no fatigue is felt.* On the day of victory, all of the effort is worth it. Although I have not yet mastered long-term consistency, Push Periods have at least allowed me to develop a work ethic that evaded me the first 19 years of my life.

Lost in thought, time flies by. I blink and before I know it, I am the next speaker on the agenda. As I look down at my speech, I shake my head realizing that the only thing that I have added is my signature about a dozen times over. Damn it.

Neil Fletcher, the District Manager in Reno, is wrapping up his message on Holiday Selling. I have known Neil for about a year, and he is one of my favorite people. Not a particularly close friend of mine, but he is the type of person who is always genuinely nice to everybody and pleasant to be around. Like

Anthony, he is also wearing a Santa hat, but it looks more fitting on Neil. He is in his late 20's, but with his boyish good looks could easily pass for a high school student. He resembles Toby Maguire, but has a build much like the pre-Spiderman Toby.

"...So make sure to wear your Santa hats, give your customers candy canes and you'll be sure put them in a great mood with your Christmas Spirit. Thanks," Neil finishes with a wave and a smile to the eager sales force before him.

As Neil walks back to his seat and Jesse takes his place at the podium, the butterflies in my stomach start to feel more like a swarm of killer bees. Trying to relax, I take a deep breath and then another.

"All right, did you guys learn some good stuff from Neil? Great. The next speaker on the program is going to talk to you about maximizing the Push Period that starts on Monday. I asked Hal to give this message because I do not think there is a more qualified person in our division, and maybe not even in the entire company, to talk to you about Push Periods. Hal started last summer in the Fresno office, and while working as a DJ on Q97, he broke the all-time Fast-Start record, selling $15,058 of Cutco in his first ten days. Then he went on to break the Western Region Push Period record, which was $12,000 at the time. Hal sold $18,036 for Summer Conference One. I'll let you think about that number for a second..." After a brief pause, Jesse continues on, "He then followed up his Summer Conference One performance with a sales report of $10,149 for

SC2. Hal finished his first six months with more than $60,000 in sales and was inducted into the Academy of Champions at this year's Kick-Off Conference. He moved up to Sacramento this summer and opened his own office, and he finished as one of the top Branch Managers in our division. Here to talk to you about how to maximize *your* Push Period, let's bring him up, Yo Pal Hal!"

A wave of applause runs rampant over the crowd. Admittedly, I love the adulation, and it is Jesse's fantastic introduction that reminds me I do have the qualifications to perform this speech. This is where I find the strength to stand up.

My heart races as I leave the safe haven that is my chair and venture out into the terrifying uncertainty behind the podium. As I set my notes down and adjust the microphone, all eyes are on me, and I can feel my perception of the audience's expectations piercing my skin like needles.

I clear my throat, look down at my notes with shaky hands and begin to speak, "I have been thinking a lot about what a Push Period really is, and what makes it different than any other two weeks of the year. What makes it special? And I came to realize that a Push Period is just a *reason*. It is a two weeklong reason for YOU to work harder, for YOU to make more money, and for YOU to show yourself and your team what you are capable of.

So, what does it take to show up at the Division Meeting with a strong Push Period? What is the difference between those who finish strong, and those who don't?

Is it belief in yourself...? Is it your sales skills...? Or is it just plain hard work...?

What did it take for me to do my best and what will it take for you? Well, when I first started, I surely did not have a lot of belief in myself as far as what I could do for a Push Period. Like I said, I was brand new and I had never even been in a Push Period. And my sales skills, what sales skills? All I knew about selling was what I learned in training. I still read straight from my training manual. But there was that last thing, *hard work*. I realized that the only thing I had total control over was how hard I was willing to work. I took that idea into consideration and I used it."

As I continue speaking, my nervousness has faded, all but forgotten. Fear has been pushed aside by momentum and I am in my zone. Now, I do not claim to be a polished public speaker by any means. I talk much too fast and my AD/HD is apparent as I constantly digress from the main point and go off on one tangent after another.

The only thing I really have going for me is my enthusiasm. I just naturally get very excited and people seem to get drawn into my enthusiasm, and before they have a chance to realize that one point may not logically lead into the next, I am already on to the point after that. I move about the front of the room with poise reminiscent of an infomercial host, though not *quite* as cheesy.

Finally, I bring my speech to a close, "Push Periods have

changed my life and a single Push Period can change yours. They have allowed me to grow as a person while expanding my capacity as a sales rep. This is possible for you when you make a commitment to put your heart and soul into these next two weeks and give it everything you have. Get ready… it's Push Period time!"

Everyone leapt to their feet and bombarded me with a wave of applause, as I looked around the room feeling overwhelmed with pride. I exhaled deeply, letting the breath flow from my lungs, relaxing for a moment and taking in the scene, enjoying every second. It is not every day that a salesperson receives a standing ovation from his peers. Yet here it was; the moment was perfect.

Our Division Manager, my boss and friend, Jesse, resumed his post at the podium, quickly wrapping up the meeting. At least, it felt quick to me. All of the tension and anxiety that had clouded my mind had finally subsided. I felt confident and relieved.

That night, I was the one who held the Push Period record for the largest sales report in the Nor Cal Division and I'd been asked to speak today, to rally the troops. Judging by the resounding applause I received, I felt confident that I'd accomplished my task.

Once outside, everyone decided to head over to Buck's Steakhouse, a nearby restaurant, for Amber's pre-birthday celebration. We arrived before the rest of our group, so we decided to pop over to the music store, across the parking lot from the restaurant, to pass some time. I had recently taken a liking to classical music. I think it was my feeble attempt to seem more sophisticated, but as frugal as I was, I was still thrilled that I could find some of the best classical CDs in the discount bins. I quickly rummaged the $3.99 tub and came out with the holy trinity of classical composers – Beethoven, Mozart and Tchaikovsky. I eagerly made my purchase and Amber and I crossed the parking lot to meet our friends at the restaurant.

Buck's Steakhouse was a fun setting for Amber's pre-birthday celebration, with an upbeat atmosphere and a rustic-country theme. The hostess pushed together a few tables in front of the window for us. As I pulled back Amber's chair for her to sit down, I saw Gloria and Jesse pull up in his gray BMW. They were followed by Jeremy behind the wheel of his forest green Ford Ranger and our assistant manager, Chris Moynihan, riding shotgun. Within a few minutes, about half a dozen other friends showed up to join the party.

The festivities began, and for the next hour everyone indulged in laughter and fun, and I was glad to see that Amber seemed to be happily eating up all of the attention. Although it was Amber's birthday dinner, most of the evening's conversation found its way onto the same topic that it usually did–*Cutco*. We Cutco reps tend to sincerely and enthusiastically love our jobs. Every time we get together, telling stories about our humorous appointments typically monopolized our conversations. Our significant others learn to love it as much as we do, either by choice or by default.

At 11:30 p.m. I was ready to go. I knew I needed a good night's sleep before the craziness of Push Period began. So I initiated the good-byes and everyone gladly followed my lead.

Jesse and Gloria sped out of the parking lot first, shouting farewells from the sunroof. I yelled goodbye to Jeremy and Chris as I opened Amber's door and then climbed into the driver's seat. I took a moment to appreciate my first new car, which symbolized for me all of my hard work with Cutco, and inhaled the intoxicating new car smell. Just then, Amber interrupted my thoughts with a sigh that could only mean, "I know what you are doing... let's just get out of here."

We were relaxed, listening to Tchaikovsky's melodies and heading home to our familiar apartment without a single worry. Spending time with my great friends just reminded me of how blessed I truly was. I felt I was living my life to the fullest, and with so much potential, it could only get better.

After that moment, my memory becomes fuzzy. Perspective is an amazing thing, each of us experiencing reality in our own unique way. I have my view of the crash and the evening that preceded it. I am sure the driver of the truck that slammed into us has his own perspective of the occurrence, as did the family in the Saturn sedan. I have asked my friend Jeremy, who arrived at the scene of the accident just minutes after the crash, to share his perspective. What follows is his recollection of *that night.*

8

A Friend's Perspective

by Jeremy Katen

"So long as we are loved by others I should say that we are almost indispensable, and no man is useless so long as he has a friend."

—Robert Louis Stevenson

Chris and I left Buck's Steakhouse in Gloria's green Ford Ranger. We were gaining speed and trying to catch up with Hal, but as he made his way onto Highway 99, we found ourselves stuck behind a red light. Chris looked at me, a little disgusted by my juvenile behavior.

"I think you lost Hal, Jeremy. You might as well slow down," he said sarcastically. Chris was always a little uneasy when I was behind the wheel. However, I was still determined to catch up with Hal on the freeway.

We cruised along the CA/99 freeway heading southbound to Fresno. There was a light fog, so I made sure to double-check in all directions before switching lanes. I was awake from all of the excitement stirred up by the evening and now armed with my newfound motivation: *catching Hal.* So I put on some rock music and increased our speed. We were about ten minutes into the drive and rocking out to an AC/DC song when I decided that my effort to catch up with Hal was futile and I should probably slow down. As soon as I eased my foot off the gas, we saw something.

I always pride myself in being one of those people who does not rubberneck or try to look at accidents as I drive by. However, tonight there were no other cars on the road and this accident stuck out like a cowboy at a rap concert.

"Dude, Chris, check it out," I said nodding my head up to turn Chris' attention to the truck dead ahead. "Looks like there was just an accident; see that crashed up truck?"

We both watched as the truck, still in slight motion, rolled back and came to a stop in the middle of the freeway. Chris and I looked at each other simultaneously. "Weird," we muttered together in unison.

I slowed down even more, confused and amazed at the site. I pulled around the truck only to find a path paved with glass and debris. After passing the truck, I kept in the left lane unsure if I should stop to see what had happened. Before I had time to finish deciding, Chris glanced over his right shoulder and noticed what looked like a white mangled car. Then, encompassed in disbelief and astonishment, he said aloud, "Jeremy, I think that's Hal's Mustang over there."

"What?" I questioned. "No way. Dude, are you serious?"

"Yeah, I think so man," he replied nervously.

I immediately made an abrupt turn onto the right shoulder of the freeway, jumped out of the truck with it still running, and asked Chris to grab the wheel as I left the car door wide open. I was overcome with anxiety and disbelief, as I focused my attention and ran to what was left of this white car. As I grew closer, my worst fears were confirmed. I could hear Amber crying and calling for Hal as she was attempting to pull herself out of the car.

I ran over to the driver's side of the Mustang, carefully helped Amber from the car, and laid her on the damp grass. "Amber, are you all right," I questioned. "Does anything feel broken?"

"No, I don't think so, but my arm and leg really hurt," she answered breathlessly as she broke into tears and pointed at the car. "Jeremy, you have to help Hal!" she screamed. "He's not moving. He is not moving. Please get Hal!"

At that moment, two other women came running up, sincerely worried, and asked what they could do to help. I asked them if they had any blankets or jackets they could give Amber to keep her warm. It was freezing cold outside, and I did not want Amber to go into shock or get hypothermia.

The women wrapped Amber in a blanket from their trunk and I asked them to stay with her, which they were more than happy to do. I stood for a moment, a little shocked myself and wondered what to do next. *Hal.* I headed toward the other side of the car, and nothing could have prepared me for the scene in front of me. The new car that Hal was so proud of was destroyed. Through the mangled mass of steel, I could see Hal, covered in blood and pressed unnaturally between the driver's side door and the Mustang's center console.

This cannot be happening, I thought. "Hal, can you hear me? Can you hear me Hal? Come on Hal, say something! Hal, groan or moan or something if you can hear me!"

As I looked down, I could see that the entire front of the car, the dashboard, the steering wheel, everything, was pressed hard against Hal's legs and chest. It was then that I noticed that Hal's ear was almost completely torn off, part of his skull had been crushed and there was blood everywhere.

A muscle-clenching shiver shot through my body, partly due to the December cold, but mostly at the unbelievable sight of my best friend. I searched around for a good place to check a pulse and was tremendously relieved when I was able to find one. I looked up at the gathering crowd, and realized that I had not even thought to call an ambulance.

"Has anyone called an ambulance?" I yelled in the general direction of the crowd.

"Yes, they are on their way," a woman answered.

I glanced back down at Hal—deeply relieved he was alive, but afraid to move him. I stepped away from the car for a moment. As I turned around to walk away, my eyes caught a glimpse of the truck that had prompted my attention in the first place.

The truck was about 30 yards away. I ran over to check on the driver. The door had been torn off, making it easy to see inside and access the passenger. When I approached the truck, I could tell he was still alive from the warm exhalation of his breath into the cold air. From what I could tell, he had hit his head on the steering wheel. There appeared to be light bleeding from just above his brow.

The man looked to be in far better condition than Hal did, and, other than being unconscious, seemed quite all right. I pulled myself together as I didn't want Amber to see me at all shook up, and I ran back over to check on her.

Once I reached Amber, all she could say was, "How is Hal?" She looked absolutely terrified, and I was afraid to tell her exactly what I had seen. "Well, I've got good news. He's not dead," I answered in a sarcastic tone. Realizing this was no time to make light of the situation, I spoke in all seriousness. "Hal's unconscious, but he has a pulse and he's going to be fine," I continued on, trying to hide my own fears with a half-hearted smile.

The second she heard me say that he was unconscious, she broke into tears again, and the women who had been sitting with her began to console her. "Amber, it's okay, honey. The paramedics are on the way. They'll be here soon," the stranger comforted.

I put my hand on Amber's shoulder to get her attention. "Amber, I know this might be hard for you," I said, "but I need you to tell me as much as you can remember about what happened."

Amber stopped crying for a moment, long enough to try to

speak. "I'm not sure," she said whimpering. "Hal and I were arguing over something, I don't even remember what, and I was trying to change the CD. The next thing I know I heard Hal yell out. I looked up and all I saw were two headlights. Then I felt this huge crash, and then another one. I think another car hit us, too. It all happened so fast. I don't remember anything after that, but what seemed like only a short time later, I remember coming to and trying to open my door, and that's when I saw you running up to the car. That's all I remember."

Then she looked down into her lap. I felt for her, but I couldn't find any words to make her feel better.

Amber lifted her head back up and started asking again for Hal. "How is Hal? Is he okay?"

"Amber, he's okay. He's just unconscious," I reaffirmed to her as calmly and confidently as I could. Truth be told, I really had little indication he would be okay. All I had was my hope.

Amber started to cry again as I headed over to Hal's contorted car to watch over him until the ambulance came.

I didn't know what else to do, so I talked to Hal, trying not to think about what had happened and what was going on. I even started playing this game called *snaps* with him. It was a silly little game that he and I would often play, in groups, to get laughs. I knew that Hal was unconscious, but I was simply trying to distract myself from the obvious and hide from my fears.

I could hear Amber's sobbing progressing into profuse

wailing. She was obviously in shock, and by the time the emergency vehicles arrived—an ambulance accompanied by two fire trucks, followed by a second ambulance and three police cars behind them—she was in total hysteria.

Before I knew what was going on, I was surrounded by firemen and paramedics. A team of men and woman in uniforms moved quickly and shouted commands at each other. A couple of them ran over to help the man in the Chevy truck, while Amber was being tended to. She was hastily led to an ambulance and driven off to a hospital in Modesto. The remainder of the crew had gathered around Hal and was working on a game plan to extract him from the wreckage he was trapped beneath.

The door to the car was completely jammed shut, and it was impossible for them to pull Hal out the passenger's side as the entire steering column was practically embedded in his lap. After a moment or two more of watching all of the action, I realized that I would be most helpful by simply stepping back and letting the emergency teams do their job.

I stepped back quite a few feet as Chris walked up to me. "How's Hal?" he asked as if oblivious to the severity of the situation.

"Oh, well he's great. He's just been in an accident, he's bleeding and unconscious. How do you think he is?"

"Hey look, I got a girl's phone number," he retorted as he stuffed his cell phone into his pocket.

"Are you kidding me?" I asked, insulted by his indifference to the current situation.

"No, see that girl over there," he pointed to a girl standing with her mom next to a car, shrugging his shoulders. "We were just talking, and I asked for her number. I mean, what else am I going to do?"

"Dude, you never get girls' numbers, and the one time you do is when my best friend is dying in his car. I know you and Hal aren't that close, but I mean, come on!" I thought for a second that Chris was probably just as shaken up as I was, and maybe didn't know how to deal with the situation.

"So, Jeremy, what are you going to do? I've got to get home. My parents are expecting me back tonight and it's pretty late. Are you going to stay?"

"Yeah, I think so. I can't just go home right now." I replied softly, unable to turn my eyes away from the Mustang.

"Okay man. I've got to get going, but call me if you need anything." Chris then turned and said one last thing as he was walking away, "Do you think you should call his parents?"

I had not even thought about calling Hal's family, but I knew that I needed to. *What would I say?*

I had no clue what I would tell them, so I decided that I should call Amber's family first. I had only met them a couple of times at our apartment, but I felt better calling them, for practice first. Amber's mom answered almost immediately, giving me little time to prepare what I was going to say. "Hi,

Mrs. Allewine?" I asked in a questioning tone, uncertain that I had reached the correct person.

"Yes," she replied a bit unnerved to be receiving a phone call so late in the evening.

"Hi, I am Hal and Amber's friend, Jeremy. I'm sorry to call you so late, but I thought you should know that they were in a car accident."

"Are they okay," she asked, her voice surprisingly calm.

"Well, yeah, kind of. I mean Amber is okay. She hurt her arm and leg, but she'll be all right," I answered. "Hal is unconscious and being pulled from the car right now. They already took Amber to the hospital, but I'm not sure which one yet. I'm sure that when he's ready, they will take Hal to the same one. I'll call you and let you know as soon as I find out which one."

"All right, that's fine. Do you know what happened?" she asked.

I relayed everything to her that Amber had told me, and then added, "I still have to call Hal's parents. I'll call you when I find out about the hospital." I wrapped up the conversation and then ended the call.

I took a deep breath, looked down at my phone and wished that I had just finished talking to Hal's parents. I found Hal's home number in my phone and hit *send*, making the single-most difficult call I had ever made. As I listened to the phone dial, I looked over and saw the firemen using the 'jaws of life' to cut into the car. I prayed to myself, "God, please just let Hal live."

Then I heard the phone ringing.

"Hello?" answered Hal's mother, who sounded as if I had awoken her.

"Hi Julie, it's Jeremy. I'm sorry to call you so late, but Hal's been," my throat was dry and I reflexively tried to swallow, "in an accident," I managed to get out.

"Wait, what?" she gasped. "Hold on, Jeremy. Here, talk to Mark," her voice muffled as she handed off the phone.

There was silence on the line, and I could tell Mark was asking his wife why she had handed him the phone. "Something about an accident, I don't know. Talk to him."

Mark took the phone. "Jeremy, what's going on?"

"Hey, Mark. Um, Hal's been in an accident."

"What happened?" Mark demanded. I could feel the fear in his voice.

I tried my best to explain the events of the evening. I told Hal's dad that Hal was in a serious car accident, and that he was being airlifted to a hospital, but I did not know which one. Mark begged me for more information, and to tell him how bad it was, but I felt so sad having to relay to him what I saw. He pleaded with me to stay with Hal, to tell him that his mom and dad loved him very much, and that they were on their way. Before hanging up, Mark said, "Jeremy, please tell Hal to hang in there. Tell him we'll be there soon."

I promised I would do just that, but I had to cut the

conversation short when the noise from a helicopter, flying low overhead, interrupted our talk. I agreed to meet Hal's parents at the hospital and clicked off my phone as the helicopter made its descent.

I realized now that Chris was gone, and I had no ride and no way to get to the hospital. Unsure of what to do, I watched as they carefully removed Hal's body from the wreckage and cautiously loaded him onto the helicopter. It comforted me to see the rescue workers take such good care of Hal, and I wanted so badly to trust that they would save him.

Not wanting to be left behind, I asked one of the officers if I could get a ride to the hospital. I explained who I was, that I had no vehicle available, and that Hal's parents were expecting me. On our way, I placed one more call to Hal's parents, informing them that Hal was being flown to Modesto Memorial Hospital, and with the officer's help, provided directions to the location as well. Then I called Amber's mom to do the same, and finally I thought to call Jesse's cell phone. He was in disbelief and said that he and Gloria would turn around, and that they would be at the hospital within an hour.

I arrived at the hospital and went to the waiting room of the emergency ward. I sat around reading magazines and drinking cold coffee until Jesse and Gloria showed up. I relayed everything that had happened, as they hung onto my every word in utter shock. Jesse kept repeating, "Oh my God, I can't believe this is happening. Oh my God..."

Finally, Hal's parents appeared with his sister, Hayley, as well as his Aunt Wendy and Uncle Mike. With no doctors in sight, they immediately turned to me for information. Hal's mom hugged me, and we sat in the lobby while I recapped the night's terrible events with them once more, answering all of their questions to the best of my ability. I could not imagine the pain that they were feeling at that moment, experiencing a parent's worst nightmare and not knowing if their son was dead or alive. We were all desperate to find out Hal's condition.

Finally, a nurse appeared and instructed us to follow him. Nothing could have prepared us for what we were about to hear and see. We were led down the hall into a small meeting room where we were told to wait. Minutes passed in silence. Then, a doctor in a white coat accompanied by a minister entered the room. He introduced himself as the trauma surgeon and wore a sorrowful expression on his face. He said that at the time Hal was extracted from his vehicle he had no vital signs, but they were able to resuscitate him, and put him on artificial life support as he was being airlifted to the hospital. He said that Hal had lost over half of his body's blood supply, and he needed immediate surgery to stabilize him as well as flush his wounds of the paint, metal, and debris from the accident. There were no promises on what the outcome would be, and Hal's future looked very uncertain.

As we were all escorted in to see Hal before surgery, I could barely walk. We clung to one another, and I could see the pain and disbelief in everyone's eyes. As we entered the trauma room, I saw my best friend's body, mangled and bloody, with tubes protruding from every which way. The back and top of his head were crushed; his left temple and eye were covered with a bloody bandage, as was his ear. Surgeons had drilled a hole in his forehead and inserted a tube to drain fluid from his swelling brain, and his perfect hair that he was so meticulous about had been shaven erratically.

Fighting for the energy to speak, Mark asked the surgeon for a summary of Hal's injuries. Hal had multiple compound fractures to his left arm—his elbow was crushed, his radial nerve severed, and his wrist dislocated. Hal's pelvis was fractured in three separate places, and his femur bone also suffered a compound fracture, which I knew to be the most severe type of break. Both of his ankles were sprained, his left lung had collapsed, his spleen was ruptured, and he was bleeding internally. Hal was badly bruised and had abrasions from head to toe. It looked as if my best friend had been beaten to a bloody pulp.

Hal's dad kissed him on the nose and told him that he loved him, to be strong, and to hang in there. We were all in shock, and I could not comprehend how Hal could possibly sustain these injuries, or how his family could survive the loss of another child.

All of us camped out on the chairs and floor of the intensive care unit waiting-room, where Mark, Julie, and Hayley would spend the next two weeks of their lives, praying for Hal's survival, and watching every breath he took and every detail of his treatments. They prepared for the many surgeries to come and waited patiently for Hal to awake from his coma.

Hal's vital signs were unstable for the next week, and I cannot recall just how many *code blues* took place, where his heart stopped beating and Hal struggled to hang on to his life. He was given four more pints of blood and underwent numerous surgeries. Just when we thought he was making forward progress, we got more bad news of another setback; Hal had developed pneumonia as well as an airborne staff infection in the I.C.U. ward. Both were potentially fatal to someone in Hal's condition.

Friends and family traveled from all over the state to visit Hal. His Cutco family, as he liked to refer to them, showed exceptional support. Our Regional Sales Director, J. Brad Britton, and his wife Paulette visited Hal's bedside, as did our Regional Vice President, Bruce Goodman, with his wife, Barbara. Vector's CEO, Michael Lancellot, sent an encouraging letter via overnight mail, which Hal's mom read aloud to him while in his comatose state. The Cutco customer service department even had a banner delivered which read, *"Get Better Soon Yo Pal Hal!"* and was signed by everyone in the department.

People seemed to come out of the woodwork to show their love and support for Hal and his family. In fact, he had so many visitors that the hospital staff informed us he had literally set a new record, having had more visitors than any other patient that had ever resided there. *Geez, even in a coma, Hal was still breaking records.*

Still, it was almost a week before Hal showed any signs of life. All of us had been encouraged by the doctors to talk to him and let him know we were there. Apparently, even in a coma, a person's subconscious registers familiar voices and communication can improve his or her recovery time.

One day, his sister, Hayley, was next to his bedside, holding his hand and telling him how much she loved him. His right eye (the one that was not damaged) began to open ever so slightly. Hayley's optimism overtook her, and she immediately called the nurse in to share what she had witnessed.

The nurse responded that it was normal for his eyes to open and close, but that he was still comatose and would likely remain that way for a long time. Still grasping Hal's hand, Hayley asked how they would be able to tell when he was coming out of his coma. The nurse said that once a patient showed signs that he or she was beginning to awaken, she could then ask them to respond in nonverbal ways, such as squeezing her hand to acknowledge the patient could hear her.

Hayley felt a gentle squeeze on her hand. Her eyes widened, "Oh my gosh, I think Hal just squeezed my hand!"

"Are you sure?" the nurse replied. "Let's try again. Hal, if you can hear me, squeeze your sister's hand."

This time there was no mistaking it, as Hal gave Hayley's hand a firm squeeze, and his eyes fluttered simultaneously. Hayley burst into joyous tears as she jumped to her feet, asked the nurse to stay with her brother and ran off to proclaim the news to Mom and Dad.

Hal continued to show signs of life and finally, on the sixth day, my best friend began to wake from his coma.

9

"CAN'T CHANGE IT"

*"The pain that you create now is always some form of
non-acceptance—some form of unconscious
resistance—to what you cannot change."*

—Eckhart Tolle

Of course, I don't remember the time I spent being
comatose, and I can only vaguely recall waking from it. I know
it happened slowly, over a period of a few days, maybe
something like coming out of hibernation. Opening my eyes, I
saw my parents at my bedside. They were crying and smiling,
both at the same time.

At first, I had little comprehension of what was going on.
My memory was cloudy, and I didn't know where I was or how I
got there. I could barely move any part of my body. As I began
to understand the shape I was in, yet couldn't remember what
happened, I was overcome with fear. Thank God my family was
there to comfort me, assuring me that everything was going to be
okay. They were my real lifeline.

One of my first thoughts was about Amber. She wasn't
present when I woke from my coma, and I was deeply worried
that she had been hurt—though I could not remember what had
happened or why I felt the way I did. Because I suffered a
closed-head injury, my short-term memory was drastically

impaired. So, I had to be reassured over and over again that Amber was okay. I'd ask about her, and then five minutes later, I would ask again. This would repeat itself continuously throughout the day. My family showed remarkable patience with me, and it wasn't until Amber finally returned to my side that I regained some feeling of certainty. But it was fleeting, for as soon as she left, even if only for short time, I would soon return to a state of panic.

The problem was that the accident damaged my frontal orbital lobe. This is the area of the brain that affects judgment, as well as short-term memory. Coincidentally, this is the area of the brain affected by alcohol, and causes the symptoms associated with being drunk. The result? I constantly behaved as if I were drunk, uninhibited and blurting out every thought as it entered my mind, good or bad.

During my time in Modesto Memorial Hospital, my mom, dad, or my sister, Hayley, stayed with me at all times. My family refused to leave my side and knew that, because of my poor memory, I would get scared and confused if left alone. I would even forget where I was.

It wasn't all gloomy, however. My parents have since told me that as I was recovering, I was quite the comedian, telling jokes in an apparent drunken stupor, and, not surprisingly, making valiant attempts to sell Cutco to all of my nurses and doctors.

Looking back, I don't remember much of what went on

during those first two weeks, but having had so many stories told to me by friends and family, I feel as if these are my own memories. It is difficult to differentiate between what is my real memory and what I only remember as a result of seeing pictures, or the repeated telling of the same stories.

My first clear recollection after the accident is of the day that my medical team decided to move me from Modesto Memorial Hospital to Valley Children's Hospital in Fresno. This move was for my rehabilitation, and my parents chose the location because Valley Children's is the same facility where my sister, Amery, had received such exceptional care so many years ago. This was also the same hospital that my family had raised money for each year in Oakhurst with the *Kid's Day* fundraiser.

I remember lying on a stretcher, being wheeled out of the hospital, and hoisted into the back of an ambulance, with family and friends to see me off. For the duration of my 90-minute ambulance ride, I was alone, for the first time since the accident, and lost inside my head. At that point, my body was constantly expending energy to heal itself, and I was exhausted virtually all the time. I think I spent most of the ride sleeping.

Now that the immediate crisis had passed, there were some simple facts in front of me. *My body had been battered and broken in a car accident, hit head-on by a drunk driver. I was in a lot of pain. My new car was totaled. My brain was damaged, and I couldn't even remember what happened five minutes ago. My left hand didn't work. I was going to spend the next year of my life in a hospital. I couldn't walk, and my doctors say it would be six months before I should even consider trying.*

Just minutes before the accident, I had the whole world in my hands. I was succeeding in my work, had great friends, and a wonderful girlfriend beside me. My family was loving and supportive, and all seemed right in my world.

It just didn't seem real. I could never imagine—not in a million years—I would ever be hit head-on by a drunk driver. I mean, accidents like this happen to other people, right? They are faceless people you hear about on the news. You feel sympathy for them while their story is being told, but by the commercial break, you're up to the kitchen to get a snack. Unfortunately, there was no commercial break in this story. I was living a horror that I had been only vaguely familiar with via the late night news and morning paper.

Here was my new reality, whether I liked it or not. My body and my mind were severely damaged, and I couldn't be sure when I would see anything beyond the hospital walls.

The most common question I get now about the accident centers on how I managed to keep a positive attitude in the face of so much pain and trauma. I'm still trying to figure that out. All I can be sure of is that it never occurred to me to do anything other than persevere and recover.

So many people face unexpected and unforgiving circumstances, and you can learn a lot about a person by how they deal with adversity. Moreover, like all of the events and situations that make up our lives, I had a choice. We always have a choice of how we are going to perceive and respond to what life throws at us. I have chosen a positive view of life for as long as I can remember. A large part of that is surely the wonderful example set by my parents and my extended family. When I have encountered discouragement from others, my instinct has been to take their opinion in stride and go ahead and do what I believe is right. This optimistic attitude, paired with my realistic view of the world, has served me well.

According to many psychologists, being a victim is a common choice for most people who have suffered a devastating accident. Taking on the victim's role gives us permission to feel badly about what happened. I certainly wasn't immune from that, especially with regard to my physical appearance after the accident. After all, everyone else felt sorry for me, and all I had to do was look in the mirror to see why.

As I settled in at Valley Children's Hospital, I began to realize the implications of my injuries. Once-simple tasks, such as going to the bathroom or taking a shower, were possible only with the assistance of others. Looking at my scarred and disfigured body, I became very insecure about whether anyone would ever be attracted to me again, and I was embarrassed by my inability to take care of myself. There were times when I felt pathetic, and as a reaction to my vulnerability, I would take out my insecurities on those around me.

Ultimately, however, deciding to be a survivor was much

easier than choosing to be a victim. The "victim" role, with its isolation, depression and constant absorption in the negative, was just a bummer. Where were the fun, laughter, and excitement in victimhood? I liked my life—I LOVED my life, and I was determined to get it back.

Someone who is already prone to taking a negative view, or who has suffered one bad experience after another, is at a serious disadvantage in the face of a crisis. Those who are pessimistic will have a habit of finding everything wrong about their situation and circumstances, rather than seeking out what's right. However, I absolutely believe that there are some strategies that can redirect us in a positive direction, helping us to become optimistic. Negativity is simply a psychological habit. Like any habit, it's easy to keep because it has the comfort of familiarity. And like any habit, it can be replaced with something healthier and more effective.

As I was recovering, I began to see that the accident could become a positive experience. I chose to be optimistic and grateful for what I had, and I constantly asked myself what I could do next that would help me improve as a person and better my situation.

As I moved into Valley Children's Hospital, the most important goal to me was to start walking on my own. While in the hospital, I was on mild painkillers. Even so, I had to motivate myself to get out of bed in the morning. I had to report to physical therapy every day by 8:00 a.m. and that motivated me to get up. First of all, I knew that I wasn't going to walk if I didn't take my physical therapy seriously. More important, however, was that I loved the staff. They were so positive and encouraging, and it was super easy for me to get them laughing. I had been in fair shape before the accident, and I was fortunate to be young and healthy. But what really gave me an edge was my mental conditioning. Working with Cutco, I learned how to set goals and keep my eye on the "prize." In this case, the prize was walking independently, and by focusing on that goal I was able to move forward, literally step by step, every day.

When someone is as damaged as I was, recovery has to be a team effort. In addition to my physical therapists and doctors, I was extremely fortunate to have constant support from my family and friends. Jesse, who had always been there to celebrate my successes, showed me just how great of a friend he was when he hung with me during some of my most difficult days. He'd roll me outside in my wheelchair to the hospital's basketball half-court, and we'd play a game of "Around the World." I'd wheel myself over to the designated spots on the court, painfully stand up, and shoot the ball. It was healthy for my state of mind as well as my body. Basketball was a sport that I had always loved to play, and playing with Jesse at the hospital gave me a sense of security, knowing that I could return to my normal life. It was comical, though; there I'd be, looking like I was in the Special Olympics, grunting as I went to make a shot with my right hand while my left hand flopped uncontrollably.

This was due to the severed radial nerve in my left arm. Eventually though, I even beat Jesse, or I wore him down with my antics, but either way, Jesse's visits—as did those of all my friends—played a huge part in my recovery.

For anyone who knows me, my excitement about visitors and my enthusiasm around the members of my medical team isn't surprising. I'm a tried and true "people" person. When I wasn't giving my nurses a hard time, I was on the phone. Here was something I could control—I'd always been able to make people laugh, and nothing about my injuries impacted my social life. In fact, while I was in the hospital, I learned about the Florence Nightingale syndrome. While I had been worried about my scarred body, my friends were teasing me about getting more girls in the hospital than they were in the real world. Not that I'd wish it on anyone, but I certainly enjoyed the attention!

I have since learned that my *ACCEPTANCE* was and is the key to real, and lasting, happiness and fulfillment. It is our *resistance* that causes all of our emotional pain. Our nature to *wish* and *want* circumstances beyond our control to be different only hurts us and never helps. Our wishing that the past were different than it actually was—besides being useless—causes us to feel pain and regret. Our wanting the present moment or circumstance to be any different than it is, causes us to feel anxiety and worry. Only once I was willing to accept my circumstances could I begin to take control of them.

This did not necessarily mean that I was going to be *happy* about my circumstances. In many cases, happiness is an unlikely and unreasonable expectation. However, there is another option—a place that is neither happy nor sad—and that place is *peace*. Happiness and sadness are emotions, which are inconstant and susceptible to changing at any moment. I am sure you can think of a time when you were feeling happy and all of a sudden something *bad* happened; maybe you got a phone call of some disturbing news. Then, in the blink of an eye, your emotional state went from happy to sad, mad, or something closer to the opposite. *Peace*, however, is constant. It is not influenced by events or circumstances, but is the space in which we can create any new event, circumstance or desirable emotion we choose.

Once I accepted life for all that it was, the good and the bad, then I was at peace. I felt no resentment or anger, nor did I wish that the accident hadn't happened to me. I was exactly where I was supposed to be; I was in a place of peace, and I was empowered to create the life that I wanted. Only then could I begin taking my life head on and creating it anew.

I spent time with my sister, Amery. I prayed and talked with her, which only heightened my feeling of peace. I thought of how my mom and dad had turned their tragedy of losing their child into a selfless triumph for so many others. I asked myself the same empowering questions that they had asked themselves so many years ago. *How can I learn from this experience? How can I use it to help others?*

Many answers came to mind once I asked myself the right questions. One of the first was that drinking and driving indeed presents very real, very devastating consequences and should not be taken lightly. Although this is common knowledge, it is unfortunate that far too many people ignore their better judgment and drive under the influence of drugs and alcohol anyway.

The more I asked myself these questions, the more I came up with answers that made me feel better. Eventually I would learn to walk again, gradually my memory would improve, and once I overcame this whole ordeal, I would be unstoppable. I was beginning to see my car accident as a tremendous opportunity for me to grow. *If I could do this, then I could do anything.*

Then I began to be infused with my passion for helping others, and ideas began to form of the different ways I would be able to utilize my accident to do this. I envisioned myself on stage, as a motivational speaker, speaking with conviction about our choice to be happy. Reminiscing back to my love for writing throughout grade school, I even had the seemingly far-fetched idea that I might someday help others by writing a book about my experience.

Therefore, I decided that fully and sincerely accepting my circumstances was the choice I had to make. As hard as it was to do, it was necessary for me if I was to transcend my emotional pain and turn my life around. So I made the decision to accept my circumstances, fully and sincerely.

It was not until later, however, by reading books such as *The*

Power of Now, by Eckhart Tolle, and *The Power of Intention*, by Dr. Wayne Dyer, that I learned about the concepts behind my choices and my understanding was broadened.

This way of thinking is easier said than done, and you may even be thinking that it is unrealistic or maybe even impossible. I, too, was skeptical at first, but I practiced and practiced until it became MY way of thinking. Eventually you can live every day of your life where acceptance takes place in your heart before a circumstance even occurs. You can literally learn to *accept life before it happens.* This means you make a decision now, to live in a way where when you cannot change something, you will automatically accept it. You must first make an agreement with yourself to be open to trying this strategy in your life. All change takes time, as does forming new, empowering habits such as *acceptance.*

Here's an example of how I applied the concept of acceptance about a year after my discharge from the hospital. I was driving to a Vector Team meeting and was running late. I merged onto the freeway and entered into bumper-to-bumper traffic. It was 7:45 p.m. and my meeting started at 8:00 p.m. I was at least 30 minutes away, which would make my approximate arrival time at 8:15. I strive to be a man of my word and being late is unacceptable to me. I was getting more and more frustrated with each passing minute. Then I noticed that my body was tense and I was developing a migraine headache. I realized that I was indeed *resisting* my present reality. I was regrettably *wishing* I had left earlier, and anxiously *wanting* the traffic in front of me to move faster. These desires were completely unrealistic, out of my control, and it was my *wishing* and *wanting* that was causing me to experience mental, physical, and emotional pain.

"Can't change it," I thought to myself. "Huh, this is a good opportunity for me to practice that whole *acceptance* thing I have been reading about." I could not change my circumstances. I was going to arrive at the meeting whenever I got there and not a moment sooner. Therefore, my only real choice was how I was going to spend the next 30 minutes in the car. Either I could be completely miserable and stressed out, spending my time wishing and wanting that I had left earlier—circumstances beyond my control at this point—or I could accept my situation and enjoy the time. Either way, I was going to be late for the meeting and I figured *I'd rather be late and happy than late and miserable.* Either way I am going to be late.

"This is a pretty easy decision," I said to myself. I reached for the radio dial and began thinking about what, in my life, I had to be grateful for. I thought about my friends and family, how much I love them and how much they love me. I experienced deep gratitude for the simple gift of being alive, and thought, *what greater joy is there than that of life!* I thanked God that I had the ability to walk, run, and even for the realization I was having. I was thankful for the fact that I had a car to drive, a job to go to and food to eat, when so many less fortunate people did not. When I finally reached my destination, I slid into the back of the meeting room smiling, feeling grateful for what I had just done for myself, and empowered that I could choose *acceptance* anytime that I wanted to. I thought, "Wow, acceptance really works!"

So, try this strategy: When you find yourself feeling stressed, angry, or overwhelmed with any other destructive emotion, ask yourself first, "Can I change anything here?" If the answer is yes, that you have the power to change you current circumstance, then take immediate action that moves you toward your desired change. Your stress will be almost immediately relieved. If no, recite these three simple, life-changing words to yourself... *"CAN'T CHANGE IT."* Then relax... take a deep breath, and be at peace.

These three magic words can be your key to unlocking the door to *acceptance*. If you will repeat them to yourself the next time you are faced with a difficult situation, they will help you take control of your emotions, and your life. These words will remind you that if you can't change your current or past situation or circumstances, then your only real choice is to accept life as it is and move on. Determine whether or not you can change the future outcome, and, if you can, make a plan and take the appropriate action to do just that.

When you begin to do this, you will find yourself overcoming many obstacles and achieving more than you thought possible. You will no longer be controlled by your circumstances, like the silver sphere in a pinball machine, bouncing off whatever life throws at you. Instead, you will regain control over your life, your thoughts, feelings, and emotions as I did. You will escape the passenger seat of life and become the driver—the captain, choosing your destinations with precision, and creating the life you have always dreamed of. And no circumstance, not even a near fatal automobile accident, will be able to derail your happiness.

The ultimate goal is to eventually reach an enlightened level of thinking in which you quite literally *accept life before it happens.* This is now how I live—I accept life before it happens. What that means is that no matter what happens to me—if I cannot change it—I accept it, then I move on. As soon as I realize that I am causing myself pain or stress in the form of anger, frustration, anxiety, or any other negative emotion caused by a circumstance that I cannot change, I need only to say my three magic words, *"can't change it,"* and all of my negative feelings are released.

If I can do it, so can you. I now wear a bracelet displaying my phrase, *CAN'T CHANGE IT*, as a reminder to accept the things in life I cannot change. This bracelet serves as a constant reminder that I can be free from emotional pain. The next time you find yourself *wishing* and *wanting* reality to be different, just say, *"can't change it"* and let all of your negative energy be released. This takes practice, but once you can accept life before it happens, you will experience a sort of *emotional invincibility,* and nothing will be able to harm your emotional well-being.

Life is like my 30-minute car ride. The one thing we can all count on is that time will pass. Therefore the question is: *How will you spend your time?* Some people will choose to live in the past, worry about the future, be frustrated with the present—*wishing* and *wanting* their reality was different than it is, and create for themselves constant emotional pain. But for you, life can be different. Next time you find yourself resisting what you cannot change, simply say, "can't change it," accept life as it is at that moment and become free from your emotional pain.

10

A Big Kid In A Children's Hospital

"I know I'll think of you often and laugh at your quirky
statements and bizarre stories. You are
definitely one-of-a-kind!"
—Nurse Wendy

It was not long before I made my presence felt at Valley
Children's Hospital. While my primary focus was on
rehabilitation, my brain injury was affecting my behavior,
causing me to act like an overgrown and inappropriate teenager.
It was as though I had lost all my inhibitions—and I didn't have
that many even before the accident.

The hospital psychologist, Dr. Lebby, sat down with my
parents and me when I was first admitted to Valley Children's to
further explain my mental condition. He used a lot of big words
and medical mumbo-jumbo, but basically the idea was that my
brain filter was broken, and I was going to say everything that
came to my mind. He said that I was not able to differentiate
right from wrong, and that the people around me needed to be
aware of this and not take anything I said personally. He warned
us that I would likely be inappropriate, offensive, and possibly
even crude.

Dr. Lebby was right; every interaction with me was
guaranteed to be full of surprises. I'm lucky my sister is still

talking to me after I divulged her high school secrets (many of which were news to my parents). I shamelessly flirted with every one of my female nurses, and even told Amber's mom that I thought she was "hot." This is no exaggeration; in fact, I simply cannot, in good taste, share all of the hilarious, yet utterly inappropriate antics that took place while I was in the hospital. With my natural sense of boundaries severely diminished, I was unable to understand where to draw the line, and literally blurted out anything and everything that came to my 20-year-old mind.

My mom, dad and sister repeatedly cautioned visitors about my mental condition before letting them enter my room. They even hung a WARNING sign on the outside of my hospital room door, but most dismissed the warning, assuring my family not to worry. But nothing could really prepare my friends and family for my uninhibited behavior. I think that those with a good sense of humor and thick skin enjoyed their visits with me. On more than a few occasions, however, I'm pretty sure that visitors were unsure of how to react to my revealing comments and left the hospital a little shaken up.

Whenever my mom, dad, or Hayley were present, at a moment when I said something inappropriate or offensive, they were quick to reprimand me. I would constantly defend myself, pleading innocently, *"What, it's true!"* I was not making stuff up; I was just speaking my mind, with no concerns about the consequences of what I was saying. One day when my parents were trying to explain to me how my behavior was inappropriate for a children's hospital, I replied, "Well there you go, what's wrong with this picture? I'm not a child, I'm 19 years old!" My parents just shook their heads and chuckled because I was actually 20.

Most of the patient rooms at Valley Children's Hospital were doubles, consisting of two beds, with two patients residing in each room, separated only by a curtain. This presented a major problem; you see, the patients that I shared my room with were children, and my inappropriate comments and behavior did not sit well with their parents. As a result, I could not keep a roommate. Time and time again, concerned parents asked the hospital's staff to move their children to another room, away from me. I went through three roommates before finding one that stuck. He was a 19-year-old former gang-member who had been shot by a police officer, and his skin was definitely thick enough for my R-rated conduct. Not only was he not offended by my behavior—he thought I was absolutely hilarious!

All in all, I felt very accepted and loved at Valley Children's Hospital, and my time there was well spent. The fact that my parents made sure I was never alone made a big difference in my recovery. With their support, I had every opportunity to rehabilitate both my mind and my body. I had physical and occupational therapy every day from morning until early in the evening. It was a lot of fun for me and I thoroughly enjoyed it. It also gave me a wonderful opportunity to develop great relationships with all of my therapists. Everyone on staff was sensitive to my condition and appreciated my positive attitude. For the most part, I think they got a kick out of my uninhibited sense of humor.

During my stay, I cultivated a very special relationship with one of my nurses, Wendy. Our first meeting was anything but ordinary, and because of the somewhat graphic nature of this story, I hesitated to include it. But I think it may be the best example of just how uninhibited my brain injury caused me to be. And as I did at the time this happened, I think I will reserve my right to play my uninhibited card, and proclaim in my defense, *"What, it's true!"* Please be warned: this is your only disclaimer.

One lovely afternoon at the hospital, I was lying in my hospital bed with my dad keeping me company, and after a few failed attempts at going to the bathroom, my dad called the staff and requested that someone help me with my constipation. They complied and assured my father that someone was on their way.

Minutes later, Nurse Wendy entered my room. She was a very pretty woman, in her early thirties, and I quickly learned that she had been divorced and had two children. She was pleasantly upbeat and seemed to have a good sense of humor. After the small talk concluded, Nurse Wendy got right down to business, as my dad sat in a chair, a few feet from my bed, and listened.

Wendy spoke in a reassuring manner and explained, in detail, the procedure she was about to perform on me in order to loosen my bowels. It required her to put on a rubber glove and using her index finger, apply a gel-like solution to the problem area.

I glanced over at my dad, whose already rosy cheeks were now glowing crimson red. Nurse Wendy also seemed slightly embarrassed, not so much for herself but for me. She said, "Hal, I want you to know that this shouldn't be weird for you in any way. This sort of thing is just part of my job, so I don't want you to get embarrassed or anything." She was so sweet and concerned with my feelings, but nothing could have prepared her for how I was about to respond.

"Well, Nurse Wendy... I know this is our first time meeting and you don't know me that well, but I just want you to know that this won't embarrass me at all."

"Oh good," she sighed.

I continued, "No, not at all. In fact, quite the opposite—this sort of thing sounds like it might even turn me on."

"Hal!" my dad shouted.

"What, *it's true!*" I retorted. Wendy sat there in shock, and my dad apologized profusely for my behavior. Nurse Wendy was surprisingly calm and cool, laughing it off as *no big deal.*

Wendy pulled the curtain around my hospital bed in order to provide us with some privacy. You can probably imagine how the next few minutes proceeded. I was reacting completely without any inhibitions or internal censor. My poor dad!

I wasn't trying to be rude or offensive, I just didn't get it. I

- 119 -

sincerely saw nothing wrong with my comments. My judgment was so severely impaired that even when my family would explain how inappropriate I was behaving, I refused to see their point of view. I argued with them until they usually deemed me *hopeless* and gave up.

Despite our awkward introduction, Nurse Wendy and I went on to cultivate a very special relationship with each other. I developed a major crush on her, and she became very fond of me, appreciating my optimism and sense of humor. And every single day, I assured her that as soon as I was released from the hospital, I would return to selling Cutco to support her and her kids. We always had many laughs, and I was grateful for her good company.

Laughter played a vital role in my healing process, as I was always looking for the humor in my everyday activities and interactions. Although I managed to stay positive, I lived in tremendous pain every single day. One afternoon, about three weeks after my accident, I was sitting up in my hospital bed, wearing my oversized hospital gown. I was talking with my friend, Matt, on the phone when my dad walked into the room. He waited patiently until I ended my call and hung up the phone. When I did, he said that he wanted to talk to me. He wore a serious demeanor as he sat by my bedside and asked me how I was doing.

"Great, Dad. Why, what's up?" I replied nonchalantly.

He expressed that he knew I was getting along okay when

other people were around, but he wanted to know how I was *really* feeling when I was alone, thinking about the accident and what had happened to me. Was I sad… angry… depressed…? I was taken aback by his questions.

He sympathized with me and said that he understood how I would feel depressed about my situation, or angry with the drunk driver. He said that any feelings that I was experiencing were completely normal, and I should not hide from them. He appeared to be deeply concerned about my emotional well-being, as any father would be.

His sincerity touched me, but his inquiry into my emotional state almost made me laugh. I was silent for a moment, unsure of how I should respond. "Dad, I honestly thought you knew me better than that! I'm awesome. Seriously. After you showed me the pictures of my Mustang, I'm just grateful to be alive. I feel like I have been given a second chance, and I know that this happened for a reason, it's just up to me to figure out what that reason is.

I've already been thinking about all of the positives that can come out of my accident. I will get through this, and once I do, I don't think there will be anything I can't do."

My dad was smiling now and looked a little relieved.

"Ever since I started selling Cutco, I have lived by the *five-minute rule; It's okay to be negative, but not for more than five minutes.* It's been a heck of a lot longer than five minutes, and so now I have to decide how I can learn from what happened and how can I use it to help other people." As I spoke, I became more and more excited. "I can't change the fact that this happened to me, but I can choose to learn from it. I will always use the accident as a reference to serve me for the rest of my life," I added, not losing tempo, "and I can already see that I can use my experience to help and encourage other people, the way you and Mom did after Amery died. I can help a lot of other people. Besides, you know that I love a challenge. I swear, Dad, stop worrying... I am absolutely fine."

My dad turned his head for a second, and I wondered if he was crying. When he turned back to look at me, I could see that he was. He smiled and told me that he loved me. He gave me a big hug—the kind that fathers give their sons when they are very proud, and then he left. I later found out there was a very specific reason my dad came in to talk to me that day...

Earlier the same morning, Dr. Lebby, the hospital's psychiatrist had asked my mom and dad if they would meet with him. He expressed some concern over my condition. He told my parents that I was *always* happy and upbeat when he met with me, cracking jokes and making him laugh every chance that I got. He said that he had been working with accident victims for years and that my behavior was not normal for someone who had been through such a traumatic experience. He conveyed his prognosis, which was that I was in denial, and he requested that my parents talk to me and find out how I was *really* feeling.

After my dad's conversation with me, he revisited Dr. Lebby

and relayed everything we talked about to him. My psychiatrist was astonished. He said that in all his years he had never seen an accident victim respond the way that I had. He told my dad that he could not believe, at only 20-years-old, I maintained such an optimistic outlook. He even declared that my attitude, and the way I viewed what had happened to me, was consistent with an accident victim *three years* into their recovery process.

"Your son should consider writing a book," he even suggested, restating that he had never known a patient that responded the way I did. I think Dr. Lebby's sheer astonishment eased a lot of my parents' fears, and gave them confidence that I was going to be okay. Not only physically, but mentally and emotionally, too.

I know that my genuine happiness and good spirits touched everyone around me... from my family and friends, to the hospital staff, and patients alike. Each day I experienced a growing appreciation for how I could choose to respond to my unfortunate circumstances. I spent significant time pondering over the coincidences that led me to the night of the accident, as well as the bitter irony of those events.

For example, had I not begun selling Cutco, I never would have been at the meeting that night in Modesto, and never would have been hit by the drunk driver. But, because of what I learned while selling Cutco, and who I became through that process, I was able to thrive during the most difficult time of my life.

I also thought about my physical condition, and how close I had come to death. Reflecting on the physical condition of my left eye, I saw the miraculous. I pondered over the fact that a car struck my driver's side door traveling at over 70 miles-per-hour, shoving metal into the side of my face with enough force to break all of the bones around my eye, yet somehow stopped millimeters away from destroying my eyeball. This kind of precise destruction could not be a mere coincidence. It had to be something much greater, and God surely was to thank for this miracle.

And though my damaged brain prevents me from remembering those six minutes I spent on the other side, I have an infinite knowing, more powerful and certain than any recollection could ever be, that I connected with my Creator. I do not remember what that experience looked like, and I cannot tell you what, if anything, we discussed, but I can promise you this: my purpose is to selflessly add value to the lives of others. To empower people to LOVE the life they have so that they can CREATE the life of their dreams—and I am committed to fulfilling my purpose each day, for the rest of my life.

11

THE MIRACLE EQUATION

"The only thing that comes between a man and what he wants is the faith that he can and the will to take action."

—Rich DeVos

My developing attitude about the situation, and the message I share as a result of it, is one of unwavering faith. You've probably heard the old adage: *everything happens for a reason.* Well, my belief has always been that these so-called reasons are not predetermined nor out of your control. Instead, the explanations underlying the sometimes puzzling events of our lives are, in fact, our responsibility to determine.

Maybe the reason my accident happened to me was so that I could learn the many lessons and share them with you in this book? No wait, I take that back—on second thought, maybe the *reason* my accident occurred is because I just have bad luck. I mean, I was picked on in school, my baby sister died, AND a drunk driver unfairly struck me, right? Which of these reasons is the right one? The answer is both, or neither... it is my choice.

Can you see how I could effortlessly have chosen the latter reason, become a victim and easily justified it? I am sure I could have even gotten plenty of people to help me justify the victim role, agreeing with my pessimism and feeling sorry for me. That does not sound so bad. I mean, hey, I would have all the attention in the world. And who doesn't love attention?

Though we can all choose to be victims of our circumstances, this choice will only provide us with temporary comfort when others are around to feel sorry for us. In the scheme of life, we must decide upon reasons for life's events that empower us to become better than we are now. To do this, we must live a life of faith. I am not trying to preach to you, I am simply sharing with you the possibility that in order to achieve what you want in your life, you must maintain unwavering faith that you can and will achieve it. Whether it is faith in God, faith in yourself, or some sort of faith in the unyielding powers of the universe, I believe that unwavering faith is a necessary component if you are to truly *LOVE the life you have so that you can CREATE the life of your dreams.*

So, if everything happens for a reason, and we have the freedom and opportunity to choose our reasons, by what means do we choose? Well, first I suggest choosing to be optimistic about your life. Optimism is the tendency to believe, expect, or hope that things will turn out well. Faith is your key to living an optimistic life—the faith that life will indeed turn out well. I always say to *expect the best and accept the rest.* Maintain unwavering faith that things will turn out well, and when they don't—which can sometimes be a blessing in disguise—simply accept it as it is. Then continue to *create consistent progress.*

Once you have decided to live life as an optimist, you can enjoy every moment and every day of your life, even in the midst of seemingly unpleasant circumstances. My goal in the hospital was to rehabilitate both my body and mind. Although it was extremely difficult, I had accepted the idea that I would not walk for at least six months. Then, one morning, about three weeks after my crash, I was escorted in my wheelchair by Nurse Wendy to take some routine X-rays. At this point in my recovery, I had practiced standing up, but my broken pelvis caused me severe pain, and I could not stay on my feet for very long or without someone else physically supporting me.

A few hours later, sitting up in my hospital bed and chatting with Mom and Dad, my physician entered the room. He said he had good news, but shaking his head he appeared to be somewhat taken back. "After looking over Hal's X-rays today, I'm amazed to see that his body is healing quite miraculously. I've already spoken with his physical therapist, Cheryl, and we are going to let Hal attempt his first step today."

You cannot imagine my elation at hearing this glorious news; I was ecstatic! "Are you serious... I can walk today?" I asked in utter disbelief. It seemed too good to be true, and my parents were equally overjoyed. Minutes later, my therapist, Cheryl, appeared and wheeled me into the rehab room. She was a petite woman and not strong enough to lift me if I fell. So they asked another therapist, Bob, who was strong enough to assist me, in case I needed help supporting my weight.

Bob rolled me up to the parallel bars, which were spaced about three feet apart and six feet in length. I leaned forward to grab hold of each side. Bob put his hands under my arms and helped me to my feet. The experience seemed almost surreal; after all, I wasn't supposed to be walking for at least another six months.

I shook off my doubt and braced myself on the bars. I can remember my determination as I lifted my right foot, inching it forward. I could feel a sharp pain shoot through my pelvis, causing my body to almost collapse. I winced in pain, but grimaced with fortitude. I was a little reluctant with my second step onto my left leg, which housed my fractured femur and 14" titanium rod. I took a deep breath, momentarily closed my eyes, and prayed for God to give me the strength to take another step forward. I looked to Bob who smiled and encouragingly reassured me, "You can do it Hal; I'm right here to help you." Like Jesse, my dad, and so many mentors throughout my life, Bob inspired the needed confidence in me. I lifted my left leg and took another step, and then without hesitation, I took another.

Not surprisingly, the steps to follow came much easier. I've found this is true when attempting any change in our lives or trying something new. The first step always seems to be the hardest one for us to take. It is for this reason that Cutco sales representatives are asked to schedule their training appointments with friends, family, and anyone who we feel will most likely purchase. This enables us to practice our presentation in a more comfortable setting. It also helped us to gain confidence in a variety of business arenas; first on the phone and then in person. When we had to make those first calls to book our very first appointments, it was always an uplifting jolt of confidence to hear them say 'yes.' By calling friends and family first, Cutco representatives are taking their first step towards their ultimate goal of success with Cutco.

The point that I am driving home is that when making any change in your life, you must be willing to take the first step. Oftentimes, people avoid change or a new opportunity altogether because they feel overwhelmed by how far away their goal is. Many who desire change lack patience throughout the process, and put far too much pressure on themselves to succeed from the very start. This causes them to fold under their self-made pressure and usually quit before they've given themselves a legitimate chance at succeeding.

Change does not have to be this way. Making a change in our lives is similar to stepping into the cool ocean on the first day of a new summer. When the water is colder than we'd like, our thoughts about the first few steps are usually painful and unpleasant. But once you are submersed, you adjust to the change; the water becomes comfortable and it feels great!

Change in our personal and professional lives is the same way. All you need to do is commit to taking your *first step* into the unknown. Once you commit to taking that first step, then see how you feel—as opposed to getting overwhelmed by the next 50 before you even take your first—then you will have the drive to make that step. Moreover, once you take your first step, subsequent steps are that much easier. Life's most difficult and rewarding journeys all start with a single step.

For the days to follow, I practiced walking in my daily physical therapy with Cheryl. Pain and fatigue often overtook me, but what I liked most about Cheryl was her ability to push me beyond my limits. One of the ways she would do this was her ability to keep me focused on my goals. One day during physical therapy, my bones and muscles ached tremendously. I eventually learned that this would be common all throughout rehab, but on this particular day, I was still naïve about the work it would take to truly heal.

On this specific day, I wanted to give up. I was exhausted. I was in pain, and I only had one rep left to do, but I just wanted it to be over. After all, how much benefit could really come from one last painful rep anyway?

I tried to remain positive, but I was tired and attempted to joke Cheryl out of her commitment to get more from me. She took my opposition in stride and was not deterred. She made me realize that although the one last rep may or may not be consequential physically, the fact that I would give up and let myself down with only one more rep to go would be mentally damaging. If I started putting up mental blocks and giving up this early in the healing process, it would just make the rest of the process that much more difficult.

Cheryl was right, and so with her support, I was able to give her one more repetition with the walker, which was being used to *re-teach* me how to walk. Over time, I quickly came to realize that the lessons I was learning had applications beyond physical rehabilitation. This was when I came up with *The Miracle Equation.* I decided that by making the choice to maintain *unwavering faith*—meaning every thought, word and action were consistent with what I was committed to—while giving *extraordinary effort* at all times, then I would be able to create miracles in my own life. So I did, and it worked. Unwavering faith combined with extraordinary effort indeed created miracles every day of my recovery.

I tucked this formula for success away with me to be used when I got out of the hospital. Anything you want in your life you can have, using *The Miracle Equation.* I have used this proven formula time and time again, in both my personal and professional life. Now, let me be clear about how I define a "miracle" in this context, and that is anything you would deem extraordinary.

In fact, everything extraordinary that I have achieved in my life, whether I was aware of it at the time or not, was made possible using *The Miracle Equation.* Looking back to my first 10 days selling Cutco, when I set the new *Fast-Start* record, this was precisely how I did it. Despite my fear of failure, my doubts, lack of discipline and everything else that *I* could have let stop me, I chose to maintain *unwavering faith* while putting forth *extraordinary effort* until the end. As a result, I was able to set the new Fast-Start record, achieving something so extraordinary that no one ever had before. In other words, I created my own miracle.

Let us take a moment to look at the two elements of *The Miracle Equation*—**unwavering faith** and **extraordinary effort**. *Unwavering Faith*—the conscious choice that your every thought, word and action will be aligned with your goal or commitment—allows you to *LOVE the life you have*, because by maintaining the faith that you can have, do, and be anything you desire, you are in control of your emotional well-being and happiness. While *extraordinary effort* empowers and enables you to *CREATE the life of your dreams*, because it is in taking massive action towards your goals that the results you desire— the life of your dreams—will become your reality.

Unwavering Faith + Extraordinary Effort = Miracles. Whatever it is that you are presently committed to—your work, school, being the best parent you can be, training for the Olympics, or creating an extraordinary relationship with someone special—begin to apply *The Miracle Equation* in your life today, and create for yourself a miraculous life.

12

FINDING SALVATION IN ANOTHER
PUSH PERIOD

"Success or failure is based on how you respond to the drama
in your life. Either it makes you tough,
or it breaks you to pieces.

—Todd Smith (a.k.a. LL Cool J)

My time in the hospital was focused on rehabilitation and getting well, but the consequences of the accident were beginning to have an impact on my family. The medical bills were piling up. Stacks and stacks of paperwork, in addition to supporting me in my recovery, became a full-time job for my parents, causing them both to take extended time away from work. The stress between Amber and me became too great, causing us to break up just before Christmas, leaving my parents with the awkward chore of going to my apartment and boxing up my belongings. My personal bills, such as cell phone and credit cards, were the least of my parents' worries and would go unpaid for many months, resulting in my credit score plummeting. The financial burden of the accident and my recovery were becoming a very real concern.

It was then that we felt the true benefits of living in a small community like Oakhurst, California. Their unexpected acts of kindness were truly awe-inspiring and deepened my faith in human spirit and kinship. Nearly everyone in town helped raise money for my personal and medical expenses.

Over the years, my family had raised more than $50,000 for Valley Children's Hospital. They were involved in local charities and were active community volunteers. I learned by their example, and even as a youngster I pitched in wherever I could. It was the right thing to do, and it also gave me that chance to personally observe the truth in the expression, "What goes around, comes around." I felt so proud to live in the company of such special people as we did in Oakhurst. Friends of our family, Glen and Sandy Moore, as well as Peggy Potter, went all over town and placed donation jars, displaying my picture, in local stores. The Elk's Lodge in Oakhurst even held the "Hal Elrod Benefit Dinner" to raise additional money.

My parents shared with me that no business owner in Oakhurst would let them pay for anything. They literally refused to take my family's money and told them that my family and I were in their prayers. It is largely due to the kindness, love, and selflessness bestowed upon my family and me, during this time, that has inspired me to choose my life's purpose: to selflessly add value to the lives of others.

Once I was given a release date from the Valley Children's Hospital, I started planning what I was going to do when I got out. I remember lying in my hospital bed and thinking about the upcoming Cutco Kickoff Conference. A far-fetched thought entered my mind, programmed in my subconscious at that point, to work hard for Push Period. Then I remember questioning whether I was being realistic. *Who am I kidding? I'm a mess; I can barely walk, my left hand doesn't work, I can't drive, and I can't even remember what happened five minutes ago. What am I thinking; I can't do that... it's not possible!*

Those words triggered in me a response, something I had heard Tony Robbins say many times: *"If I can't, then I must!"* My human nature was overtaken by my nature to be an achiever, and my thought process quickly changed. I thought *I do not know anyone in the world who would try to go back to work after what has happened to me. Could I actually do it? How would I do it? Anything's possible! Okay, time to make a plan...*

I was immediately inspired by the immeasurable challenge of going out and working for Cutco during the upcoming Push Period. I decided that I could go back to work. I just needed to strategize a plan to make my goal a reality. I made an agreement with myself that if it were possible for me to work, then I must.

I did not have a lot of time. The Kickoff Conference was coming up in San Francisco in just a few weeks and I wanted to attend. I wanted to see all of my friends and colleagues who had meant so much to me. I knew that if I wanted to stay focused and inspired, I had to find a positive influence and someone to share my goal with. First, I told Jesse; then I called J. Brad Britton, my Regional Sales Director, someone who had helped to encourage and mentor me throughout my Cutco career. He was happy to hear from me, and after catching him up on my progress, I came right out and asked Brad how much he thought it would take for someone to win a trophy at the conference. He replied nonchalantly, "Gee, I don't know, Hal, somewhere between $3,000 and $4,000. *Why?*"

With unfounded confidence lending strength to my voice, I replied, "Because Brad, I am going to stand on stage and accept a trophy from you at this year's Kickoff Conference!"

J. Brad tried to talk me out of coming back to work so soon, and reassured me that Cutco did not need for me to sell any knives right now, but just to focus on getting better. What he did not realize was that I needed to sell knives to get better. I had to get back to my routine of setting and achieving goals. This was my newest goal, possibly my most difficult, and I was determined to achieve it.

Shortly thereafter, my parents brought me home from the hospital. My body was healing and I still needed anywhere from 14-16 hours of sleep each night. My waking hours were lethargic and I found it difficult to muster up the energy I needed to schedule any appointments. With four days left in the two-week Push Period, I received a very important phone call from Jesse. He encouraged me to simply make a few phone calls, then see how I felt. Rekindling my faith and ambition, he reminded me that, *"on the day of victory, no fatigue is felt."* I knew he was right. After all, when I had achieved my goal of breaking the Fast-Start record, I did not feel tired or exhausted, although I had worked so hard on so little sleep. Instead, I felt energized and more alive than ever before.

Like so many times before, a little faith and encouragement from a friend was all I needed. I could do this. I hung up with Jesse and started calling to schedule appointments. I told my clients that I would like to come over and sharpen their knives and show them new products. This gave me the opportunity to provide them with an added service and to re-educate them about Cutco.

My mom and dad selflessly took turns driving me around to my appointments for the next four days. I was still experiencing a lot of pain in the mornings and found it difficult to get out of bed. I was also still very weak and would occasionally nod off or completely lose my train of thought. During many of my appointments, I would completely forget what I was talking about and turn to my mom or dad for guidance. It was a difficult four days. However, I maintained an *unwavering* faith that I could do it, and put forth *extraordinary effort* every day until the last.

My mom and dad, along with Hayley, accompanied me to the Kickoff Conference. We sat at a round table just in front of the stage; I was so happy to be back amongst my Cutco family. The wrap-up speech for the first night addressed the topic of overcoming adversity and was given by Bruce Goodman. Much like the *Chicken Soup for the Soul* series, his message was a collection of inspirational stories. As he neared the end of his talk, he revealed that he had one more example to share of someone overcoming great adversity.

"My last story is one that is dear to many of our hearts. As most of you know, the person I am speaking of is Hal Elrod. For those of you who do not know Hal, I wish to share the incredible story of this extraordinary young man..." Bruce went on to share my accomplishments with the audience, then went on to tell them about the accident, and how I had spent the last two months of my life in the hospital. He had everyone's full attention. The room was silent. I looked around and saw many people in tears. My mom and dad were crying as well, and I began to get emotional.

Bruce finished with this, "Doctors told Hal he wouldn't walk for a year, but ever since I have known Hal, he has not been one to be limited by what people told him he could or could not do. He is, in fact, here tonight and joined by his father, Mark Elrod, his mother, Julie, and his sister, Hayley. Well, not only is it a miracle that Hal was able to walk into the room tonight, I also heard a rumor... I'm having trouble even believing this could be true, but I heard from Jesse that Hal actually went out, did appointments, and sold for the Push Period. Now, I don't know if I believe that; I guess we'll have to wait and see tomorrow morning at the count-up.

Before we commence for the evening, I'd like to officially dedicate this weekend to Hal Elrod, who has shown us by his example, that anything is possible."

I was honored by Bruce's words, and could not be more

grateful that I had the support of the Cutco family. That night, I felt how much I mattered to the people that—next to my family—I respected and cared about most. The next morning, I limped up onto the stage for a familiar count-up. I stood up there for quite awhile, ultimately accepting the fourth place trophy at the 2000 Western Region Kickoff Conference, having sold just over $7,000 in those last four days of Push.

Considering the circumstances and emotions involved, this became, by far, the proudest moment of my life. It was the day of victory Jesse had described, and he was right that not a trace of fatigue could be felt. Had it not been for Jesse's encouraging phone call, I probably would not have scheduled one appointment, or sold a single knife to anyone. So, I urge you to take an active role in your friends' lives—especially when they're down—and support them in creating the life of *their* dreams... because their success is your success, and their happiness can be your happiness.

I hope you are beginning to see that you can have, be, and create anything you want in your life. If I can do it, you can do it. It takes hard work, for sure, but very few things worth having come easy. Whatever you see as *your* personal day of victory, the journey will at times be challenging and you may feel like giving up; but know this: *On the day of victory, no fatigue is felt... On the day of victory, it was all worth it...* ***On YOUR day of victory, all of your dreams come true!***

13

BACK ON TOP

"Our greatest glory is not in never falling,
but in rising every time we fall."

—Confucious

After the Push Period, my family was forced to make some difficult changes. My mother and father began losing money with our Oakhurst Market. A large chain grocery store opened up in town, and our small mountain community just wasn't big enough to support both businesses. Unable to find a buyer for the market, my parents ended up leasing the grocery store to another family, and because our house was part of the grocery store, that meant selling the house as well. With the amount of care that I required, this financial stress couldn't have come at a worse time for my parents.

Desperate to make ends meet, Dad started driving a tow-truck for a local towing business, and Mom interviewed for a position as a flight attendant for Horizon Air. Some of her friends and family told her that she was a bit older than airlines liked to hire, and I think that challenge motivated her. She confidently told the interviewer that he would be crazy not to hire her, and that she would be the absolute best employee Horizon would ever have. Needless to say, she got the job and was required to relocate to Seattle. Mom and Dad made another difficult decision, and that was to live in two different states so that Dad could take care of me until I was back on my feet.

Since I was still in the process of healing, couldn't drive, and took physical therapy three times per week, Dad decided to rent an apartment with me. We found a place right next door to the Cutco office so I could be involved again.

During my stay in the hospital, food became one of my only vices. I had eaten pizza and chicken strips almost every day, and I found myself getting chubby. I made a decision to get back in shape, which, with my physical handicaps, wasn't easy. I spent the first few months waking up every morning by 6:00 a.m., doing 100 jumping jacks, and then taking a painful stroll down to the apartment complex's swimming pool where I would swim 20 laps. I did this exercise routine seven-days-a-week, as well as cut soda and other sugary and fattening foods out of my diet. And wouldn't you know it; with a little consistent exercise and slight improvement in my eating habits, my chub started melting away!

As spring turned to summer, I grew anxious to return to my job selling Cutco. With no car and no driver's license, I was faced with a challenge. The solution took some creativity, but I came up with an approach that worked. I invited newer Cutco reps to field-train on my appointments. I would walk over from my apartment to meet them at the office, and then they would drive me to my appointments and take notes during my presentation. Thanks to my prior success, they were eager to watch me in action, and I was grateful for their help.

Seeing my parents taking chances and making changes in their lives compelled me to think about my own goals and what I wanted in life. It was at this time that one of my best friends, Matt Recore, called me from San Francisco. Matt worked for Cisco Systems and was asked by one of his clients if he knew anyone that had proven sales ability. Winterlink was a growing technological company in need of a good sales guy, so I decided to try it. I loved Cutco, but a new opportunity sounded very enticing.

In mid-July, I prepared myself for a job interview. I knew that Winterlink required a four-year degree and at least two years of selling technological equipment for their sales reps. So, at first, I didn't believe I had much chance of getting the job. But one night while talking to my mother on the phone, she told me that I should do exactly what she'd done during her interview at Horizon Air. She told me to go in there and tell them with absolute certainty that I would be the best sales rep they would ever hire.

When I went into the interview, I did just that. I told them that I had been the top sales rep in my office ever since the first day I started, and that I would hold the same status at Winterlink. Once again, I was able to transfer my confidence and enthusiasm, and much to my amazement, I got the job!

I was to start in mid-August, and I still had not taken my driver's test, which was scheduled for later that July. I took the test on July 23 and passed with flying colors. On July 25th, I bought a black Nissan Xterra SUV, mainly because my parents insisted on me getting a larger vehicle.

By July 31, my father was making his plans to move up to Seattle. My new job started August 15, so on the 7th, I packed all my things and drove up to San Francisco. The plan was for me to stay with Matt while I got acclimated to the new city.

My first day of work away from Cutco was not what I expected. Winterlink was a fine company. However, when I was at Cutco, I was used to a more personal atmosphere with my clients. At Cutco, when I would visit a customer, it wasn't unusual to leave their homes with hugs and well-wishes. In my new job, however, all of my interactions with customers were over the phone. I was teamed with a man named Jason Born as my sales partner. For my first three days, I watched and learned from Jason. He was a funny guy and an excellent salesperson, and although we got along fabulously, I still missed my friends and family.

The evening after my second day at the new job, my pal Frankie Ordoubadi called and asked me if I had heard the news. I had no idea what news he was referring to, but he sounded as if he were concealing the code to Bill Gates' bank account. He told me that Jon Berghoff—the same Cutco rep who broke my Push Period record with a $26,000+ report last summer—had just broken his own record, showing up at this year's Summer Conference 2 with over $69,000 in sales! Not only did he break his own record, he shattered it. I was blown away. I had talked to Jon at a couple of conferences, but I did not know him that well. I decided I had to talk to him, so I got his number and called.

I wasn't jealous or angry, but the report he posted was so far beyond my comprehension that I had to know how it was done. As soon as Jon answered the phone, I reminded him who I was and told him I wanted to know if the rumor was true.

He just laughed and easily replied, "Yeah, I'm kind of a knife nerd!"

I begged him to tell me how had accomplished such a feat. He said that he didn't sleep, didn't eat, and just worked. His response reminded me of my own Fast-Start. He did 70 appointments during the two-week Push Period. For the next hour we talked about what I was doing, what he was doing, and our plans for the future. He suggested that I should leave my new job and come down to San Jose to sell Cutco with him.

I went to work the next day and reminisced, longing for my old job. I had ventured in search of greener grass, when I was living in the Emerald Forest all along. Cutco was my family. They were my best friends. I loved everything about the company and the experience working for them. I loved every one of my clients. I looked forward to talking with them, to being with them in their homes and sharing their lives. After only four days with Winterlink, I made a difficult decision to return to doing what I loved. It was a difficult decision because of the expectations that were on me, but it was the easiest decision I ever made when following my heart.

By the first of October, I had moved to San Jose and was sharing a room with my new pal, Jon Berghoff, and although we hardly knew each other when he asked me to move in, we were fast to become the best of friends. We even signed up for college courses together at DeAnza College, where I studied anthropology and business.

I went back to work at Cutco. Jon was the number-one sales rep in the country, and I was lucky to have met him. I had been fortunate in my Cutco career in that I had always surrounded myself with excellence. When I started out, Jesse was the number-one District Manager in Vector, I was now rooming with the company's top sales rep, and moving to San Jose I was joining what was then the top office in the company. I have found that it is kind of hard not to succeed when you surround yourself with such successful people. Unfortunately, the opposite is also true; it is exceedingly *difficult* to succeed when you surround yourself with people who are not committed to succeeding themselves.

I decided in late October that my new goal was going to be to sell over $100,000 for the year. I had never lived in San Jose and I didn't know anyone in the area, so I needed a jump start to get appointments. Cutco offices retain what are known as *pink slips,* which are receipts of all the customers who have purchased Cutco in any given territory. I went through all the pink slips at the San Jose office, calling customers and setting up appointments, known as *service calls,* to come by and sharpen their knives.

One of the benefits of ordering from Cutco is the service we provide long after the sale is made. All Cutco knives carry the famous *Forever Guarantee,* which includes free lifetime sharpening, and guarantees that customers will be happy with their product every day, forever.

While I followed through on this commitment to excellence, my customers were able to look through Cutco's most recent prospectus while I made suggestions on new products that might fit well into their lifestyle. Then, after servicing their knives and helping them place an order, I was able to get referrals which they happily offered since they were already satisfied customers. Cutco customers can be as fanatical about the Cutco product as our reps. So much so, that when I'm hearing a testimonial from an avid Cutco owner, I sometimes find myself joking, *settle down, they're just knives.*

My first week in November, I did $10,047 in sales. In my second week, I did $10,958 in sales and in the third week I did $3,158 in sales.

Also at that time, I fulfilled a long-time dream to meet one of my heroes, and signed up for my first-ever, live, Tony Robbins seminar. The seminar was set for the first week in December, and would take five days away from my seemingly impossible goal of selling $100,000 for the year. What I didn't realize was that those five days were going to make the difference for me.

Before attending the event, I had looked at my $100,000 goal and mentally given up, deciding that it would be just too difficult. By the time I left the four-day conference, I was reenergized to reach my goal. I needed over $30,000 in sales for the last three weeks of December, which meant I would have to average three consecutive weeks of over $10,000 each. In the history of Cutco product, no one had ever had three consecutive weeks of selling $10,000. Despite all the fantastic salespeople Cutco had employed over the past 50+ years, it was a feat no one had yet achieved. However, I was now as invigorated to accomplish it as I had my other goals. I climbed *Mt. Fast-Start* and *Mt. Push Period*, and now I wanted to complete my journey and come back from my accident with a flurry. It was obviously not about the money; more than any time before, it was about me regaining my confidence, and letting go of the insecurities that had plagued me in the hospital. I needed to prove—to myself, to Cutco, to my parents—that the accident did not define who I was or who I was choosing to be. It was my choice to make.

And so I worked. For those last three weeks, I pushed myself in the field as hard as I did in the hospital during my recovery therapy, and harder than I ever had in Cutco. Logically, it was not probable that I would be able to sell over $10,000 for three weeks in a row. It was not reasonable to expect that of myself, or to even believe that it was possible. But I had already seen miracles created in my life, and this was one more I was committed to. So, I did what I knew to do—set my intention in place, maintained unwavering faith and gave extraordinary effort every single day. I shared my goal of selling $100,000, and $10,000 for three weeks-in-a-row, with every one of my customers. I also committed to a new goal, one that was very meaningful to me, which was to follow my parents' example and donate a portion of my Cutco sales that fall to Valley Children's Hospital. My passion was contagious and my customers inspired.

I set a new company record with three consecutive weeks over $10,000 in sales. This is a record that still stands today, almost six years later. I surpassed my annual goal, selling $106,000 for the year. I also donated $2,000 to Valley Children's, and when Cutco heard the news, they sent an additional $1,000 to the hospital.

The year that began with me lying in a hospital bed ended much differently. Doing this earned me the company trip, as well as a fantastic income for a college student, but more than anything I earned the right to be proud of myself. The culmination of the year, a year in which I reached a nearly impossible goal, was testament to the fact that when you are taking life head on, everything is possible.

14

HAPPINESS IS OUR CHOICE

—Katie's Letter—

"The more we depend upon conditions outside of ourselves for happiness, the less happiness we will experience."

—Paramahansa Yogananda

People always ask me if I was *like this* before the accident. Neither my parents nor my teachers taught me the power of a positive attitude. Who I was when the accident occurred is largely because my personality prepared me to respond positively to Cutco's training and culture. The people and programs I interacted with opened my eyes to a bigger picture of life and taught me the value of positive thinking.

My success the year after my accident was no *accident*. It was the result of a conscious choice I made to be happy. All of us are striving for the same goal---to be happy. Happiness is what everyone is working for, is it not? We work, we go to school, we enter relationships all because we want to be happy, and we sincerely believe that these things will make us happy.

The challenge that people face is that they tend to let their happiness be influenced or even determined by events and circumstances outside of their control. We think that if we get more things or do more stuff, then we will be happy. I believe that this elusive chasing of happiness is ultimately disempowering and will inevitably keep people from being happy.

Here is an idea: Why not be happy all of the time? Regardless of your circumstances or your situation in life—no matter what happens to you—be happy, just for the sake of being happy. When you think about it, what greater joy is there than life itself?

What if I told you that there is no way to happiness; *happiness is the way.* It is to be chosen before your day begins and not dependent on what happens. Right now, you may be thinking that this is easier said than done or maybe even that it's just not possible. I assure you, it is possible, and I will tell you exactly how to go about it in your own life, starting right now.

You cannot always control what happens to you, but you can control how you think and feel about what happens to you. A couple of years ago, I realized that happiness is definitely my choice and a choice that everyone can make. Life is not perfect. There will always be challenges and failures, disappointments and undesirable circumstances; things will go wrong. However, if you are happy and clear-headed when problems arise, you will be in a much better state of mind to come up with solutions than if you let yourself become overrun with negative thoughts and feelings.

Below are three letters, which were a correspondence between Katie, a college student who worked for Vector Marketing at the same time I did, and me. I am sharing these letters because I think that everyone can relate to Katie and many of the feelings that she experiences. The emotions she shares are fairly common for all of us, and she raises some interesting arguments against my way of thinking.

All I ask is that you read these letters carefully, and if you can relate to Katie's feelings and emotions, please consider my response to her, as if it were written to you.

Katie's Letter:

Hal,

I have always found your story to be truly amazing and inspiring. As a Field Sales Manager with Vector, I have had the opportunity to hear you speak at conferences and other events. I just want you to know that I have the utmost respect for you and consider myself fortunate to have heard your motivational talks firsthand. Having said this, I have a few questions and concerns of my own that I would be interested in hearing your opinion on.

Recently, I stumbled across your website, www.yopalhal.com and read your motto "Happiness is a choice – I choose to be happy." I thought about that statement for just a moment before coming to the conclusion that happiness is not a choice at all, but rather the result of a decision made prior to its outcome. In your case, you chose to survive. You wanted happiness in your life, so you decided to fight for it. Having reversed this role, you could have easily given up and wallowed in your own sorrow and self-pity, but you didn't. My point? For many people, happiness is a challenge—I do not know any one person who does not want to be happy, yet so many of us are sad. No matter how much I try to cast away my depression and be happy, I simply can't win. What is your explanation for this conflict? Sometimes I wish I could ignore my depressive states, but instead I find myself in a snowball of antagonizing thoughts and overwhelming sadness.

Hal, I do not wish to derail you in any way, but I know that I would like to be happy more than anything, but I simply am not. I think for many people becoming depressed has much more to do with their body's chemistry and makeup. For some, they can become successful in overcoming great trauma. But for others, where no trauma has even occurred, being happy is a luxury that is altogether a foreign emotion. You do not decide emotions: whatever emotion a person may feel, is not their fault that it is there, nor is it their choice. In a state of happiness and contentment, I cannot simply choose to suddenly become sad. That would never happen, because even if I did think of reasons why I should feel sad, the happy ones are obviously going to outweigh the sad ones, since I was already in a great mood. On the same note, when I am depressed, I cannot up and decide that I will "feel happy today." I might be content with thinking positive things for a few moments, but again, (in this case) the sadness will overcome.

Happiness is a choice. If this is true, then why can't I win? Someone once told me that for every negative thought a person

may have, it takes five positive thoughts to even things out. I
suppose for some people, this tactic might work. But for me, I
think that bad things far outweigh the good.

Thanks anyways,

Katie

My Response:

Katie,

I really appreciate you taking the time to write me, and thank you for your kind words and honesty. You write very well and your thoughts are very insightful, so I will attempt to do justice to your inquiry.

You are absolutely right; no one can just snap their fingers and be happy. It's not that easy, but it is simple if you know what to do. I will humbly tell you what I've learned about being happy and what has worked for me.

Much in life is simply a matter of perspective. It's not inherently good or bad, a success or failure; it's how we choose to look at life that makes the difference. You can't always control what happens to you, but you can absolutely control what you think and how you feel about it. Don't believe me? Listen. You mentioned that you find yourself in a snowball of antagonizing thoughts and overwhelming sadness. Well, is it not possible then, that your thoughts (which you do have complete conscious control over) cause this sadness? So how can you think new thoughts? Well, you have to develop new, empowering habits, ones that make you happy. Take a moment and think about when you are depressed. What are your thoughts? Are you thinking about how grateful you are for all that you have in your life, how much you've accomplished, how many people love you, and how much joy, opportunity, and love awaits you in your future? Or are you thinking other thoughts, depressing thoughts? My guess is that you are consumed with thoughts about your inadequacies, faults, shortcomings, negative circumstances, etc. Because you see, Katie, everyone has both. If I always chose to think of the latter, of course I'd feel bad. I would be depressed just as you or anyone else would. I'm sure you don't think that the happy people are only those who are perfect without any faults or shortcomings, do you? Of course not, the difference is how they choose to see their life.

Negative people often justify their negativity by saying that they are being realistic. I like to think of it this way: In life we have two pages to read. One page lists everything that is positive (all that we have) and makes us feel good; the other page lists everything negative (all that we lack) and mostly hurts us. Both are *reality*, both are real and true, but which one we choose to focus on most often determines how we feel most of the time. Like I said, if I were to focus on, think about, and dwell on my faults all day, and on the problems in my life, then I will surely end up depressed. Katie, we CHOOSE our thoughts, you just have to be conscious about your choices and not let your mind wander, or your thoughts get away from you. It's like anything in life you want to be successful at: you have to work consistently at it. Remember that in life, *extraordinary results require extraordinary effort!*

I hope this letter gives you a new perspective on happiness and can help you in some way to be happier. Again, we can't just snap our fingers, so don't expect overnight results, but after awhile, your conscious efforts to be happy will become a part of *who you are,* and then it won't take effort anymore. I promise, I've done it. Good luck on your journey, and please let me know if you ever want to talk or need anything.

Your friend,

Hal

Katie's Final Thoughts:

Hal,

Thank you so much for listening to me and for taking my words seriously – I really appreciate it. Somehow, you were able to turn my backwards way of thinking around so that I have a new perspective on the way I think and the way I rationalize my thoughts.

We do have complete control of our thoughts; you are right. Whatever thoughts we choose to focus on, whether they are negative or positive, will determine how we feel in the end. It is completely my fault that I have chosen to focus on what is wrong, instead of what is right. However, I cannot justify or find a reason why I made that decision, other than maybe the bad things are easier to believe, and, therefore, easier to dwell on. Honestly, that is not even what is important in this matter. What's really important is that I start doing something now to rectify the situation.

I guess you could say that happiness is your ultimate goal, and choosing to focus on the positive aspects of our lives, as well as stopping the snowball of negative thoughts, are choices we must make to realize that goal.

One reason that I find all of this complicated is that happiness should not be this much of a fight. In the whole scheme of things, what do I really have to be sad about? Not much, yet I still am. That's why I doubted your motto. If happiness really is a choice, and I realize that that statement is true, yet I am still not happy, what am I missing here? Your thoughts and input on this were so encouraging and comforting, because I can see now that we must make a conscious decision to focus more on what's right in our lives than on what's wrong. Having realized this, I am excited to develop these new empowering habits, and, like you said, it probably will take time, but it is time that I am willing to commit to.

Hal, thank you for taking the time to read my letter and putting so much thought into your response. It truly meant a lot to me. Your passion for life is contagious, and I wish you the best in all that you do.

Thanks again,

Katie

Katie's letter opened my eyes. Though for me the concepts I learned through my experiences seemed obvious, it unfortunately is not so for everyone else. Happiness takes work. The question is, do you believe that happiness is *your* choice? I have found that most people do not, at least not at first. They make excuses for why they are not happy. *How can I be happy when I don't have a job?* Or... *How do you expect me to be happy when the person I love doesn't want to be with me?* Or... *How can I possibly be happy when my car is broken and I can't get anywhere? It's not even my fault!*

I have heard every excuse in the book, and seen many people live their life as an *everyday victim,* drawing negative attention to themselves through their constant complaining and blaming circumstances for their poor attitude.

Therein lies the eternal struggle for many people; they do not take responsibility for their happiness. Instead, they blame their unhappiness on external factors such as other people, problems, or situations. People choose to believe that their circumstances decide whether or not they can be happy. They believe that happiness is out of their control. This is simply not true. No one has to live as a passenger on an out-of-control emotional roller coaster.

(Note: Of course, I'm talking about average people here, not about people who are suffering from mental illness. They face more challenges than reading any book could solve, and there are many valuable and important medical resources for these individuals. If you are at all concerned that you are experiencing serious symptoms of depression, I urge you to contact a mental health professional.)

Let me ask you this; do you ever have bad days? What makes them bad? What if I told you that you never have to have a bad day again? Seriously, you can choose to never have a *bad* day again. It is all a matter of perspective. What most people think of as bad days, I call *character-building days*. When I have a bad day, I seek to find a lesson to be learned. If you can find some way to learn and grow from your difficult experiences, using them in your future as points of reference, then every experience will serve you well. They will actually have a positive impact in your life and build your emotional muscle, so that you can be ready to handle anything life throws at you.

Here is an example of using an experience as a reference in the future that you can probably relate to: Most of us have had our heart broken by a boyfriend or girlfriend at some point in our young adult lives. At first, you probably felt as if the world had ended and that things would never get better. You may have even told your friends that you did not see how life could go on, but it did, and, eventually, you were able to move on. That experience became a point of reference for you, something that you can draw from in the future, at times when you need that strength. The next time you are in a relationship that comes to an end, you will be better equipped to handle the situation and to deal with your emotions. It doesn't mean that it will be easy, but certainly easier.

Like anything else, this strategy takes some work. You have to want to change your thinking, and you have to commit to being conscious of what you are allowing yourself to focus on. When you have a bad day, you really have to stop and ask yourself, "How can I use this in the future?" Eventually, after doing this enough, it will become second nature and one of your personal empowering habits.

However, to practice these beliefs, you will need to be prepared for the naysayer. These are the people who will tell you that you cannot do something. "You can't get into that college... You will not be promoted... There is no way he/she will even talk to you." I'm sure you know people like this or, heaven forbid, it is you! Remember, it is never too soon to be who you are becoming and make the necessary changes.

It is unfortunate that many of us have been bombarded with these kinds of negative statements. We have friends, family, acquaintances, teachers, coaches, co-workers, and bosses who sometimes tell us what we can't do and we believe them because we trust them. Do not listen to them. I know that this is easier said than done, but look at my life and know that you can create anything of your own.

This is all a matter of perspective. I would never claim that any one of my views are *right*, they are just *possibilities*. It is up to you to interpret my ideas and strategies, and then make intelligent decisions for yourself. Listen to your heart; it holds all of your truth.

Happiness is in you; it is not hiding in a new car, boyfriend, girlfriend, good grades, or promotion. And it is definitely not waiting to show up tomorrow. It is available for you today—this very moment—and it comes from within. **There is no way to happiness;** *happiness is the way.*

15

HALL OF FAME

*"Although actions speak louder than words, it is
our intentions that reveal our soul."*

—Yo Pal Hal

In September of 2004, I reached the pinnacle of success in Vector Marketing, the *Hall of Fame*. Surpassing $500,000 in Cutco sales, I became the 16th person in the 55-year history of the company to achieve this honor, and at 25, I was also one of the youngest. My induction ceremony would take place in Las Vegas, Nevada, during the first evening of the Western Region's annual *Conference of Champions*. For this special occasion my family would be in attendance – Mom, Dad, Hayley, and even my grandma flew in from Colorado. I was so excited!

The Alexis Park Resort was the perfect setting for my Hall of Fame induction, as it represented so many memories I had from my six previous Conference of Champions. In addition to my family and fellow Cutco colleagues, many of my closest friends from home made it, too.

Entering the banquet room that night with my family was somewhat surreal. We arrived 15 minutes early and immediately located the special table at the front of the room that had been reserved for *'Yo Pal Hal and Guests.'* I helped my grandmother, and then my mother, into their seats before taking mine. Soon we were joined by Jeremy, Teddy, and Matt. Jesse had his own table directly next to ours.

Pleasant jazz music filled the room as attendees found their tables and I calmly thought to myself, *everything is perfect.* Noticing the dazed expression on my face, my dad leaned over and squeezed my arm, "Hal, this is so exciting! You're awfully quiet; aren't you excited?"

"Huh? Oh, yeah, absolutely! Sorry, Dad, I was just thinking." That was not entirely true. I was not *just thinking*; I was also *feeling* – overwhelmed with strong feelings and emotions, ranging from nervousness to ecstasy. Gratitude was at the forefront, feeling grateful for my life and the countless blessings bestowed upon me. I was relieved that the hard work it took to get me there was over, and I felt deep love and appreciation for my family, as well as everyone in the room. Despite my outward appearance being relatively calm, deep down I was concealing a ball of explosive energy. This night meant so much to me and was the culmination of the last six years of my life – tragedies and victories, failures and successes. Looking back on all that had happened to get me to this point, I shook my head in disbelief, wondering how I had made it.

I pondered over all the friends and colleagues who had contributed to this moment. It was my moment to enjoy, but I wouldn't have been there had it not been for the countless souls that had blessed my life. I looked over at my family, they were laughing at something someone had just said, and I felt myself getting choked up. How close we had come to losing each other. I closed my eyes and silently thanked God. Then I opened them wide and took a deep breath, shaking off my sentiment and praying for the strength to keep it together tonight. I did not want to break down in tears during my 'Thank You' speech.

My thoughts were interrupted by the arrival of dinner. I finished my food before everyone else, somehow thinking that the quicker I was done, the sooner my Hall of Fame induction would begin. Eventually the rest of the room caught up with me and the hotel staff came around and cleared away the dishes. Then the program got under way.

J. Brad Britton began to speak into the microphone, "Welcome to the 2004 Western-Region Conference of Champions. Tonight we will be recognizing our top achievers for their accomplishments this summer, and we have a special ceremony this evening for Mr. Hal Elrod, who will be receiving his induction into the Cutco/Vector Hall of Fame. Hal is seated right here at his table in the front, and is accompanied by his family and a few of his closest friends, who have joined him to celebrate this special night."

J. Brad continued setting the stage for the weekend. As soon as he made the last of his announcements, the two immense screens that framed either side of the stage lit up with the words, HALL OF FAME. My heart began to beat faster. Brad went on to explain the qualifications it took to reach Hall of Fame as a Sales Representative; then he described the prizes that came with the milestone: A trip for two anywhere in the world, my picture on the *Wall of Fame* at the Cutco factory in Olean, New York, one exceptionally large Hall of Fame trophy, the Hall of Fame ring, which was set in 10-karat gold and housed 11 diamonds, and what was considered by many to be the most coveted prize of all, the treasured *Book of Letters.* This book was filled with letters of congratulations and sentiments written by anyone who chose to do so, from the CEOs and executives of both Vector and Cutco, to my Region, Division, and District managers as well as my fellow sales reps. This was, in my mind, truly an invaluable keepsake.

Brad went on to highlight my career, beginning with my Fast-Start and listing the various sales records that I had broken. I took a moment to look at the expressions on my Mom and Dad's faces, and was pleased to see that they were smiling from ear to ear. Soon enough he began detailing the events and circumstances of my car accident and the comeback that followed. He used pictures to aid in the presentation, and when those of my mangled Mustang lit up the screens, gasps were heard throughout the room. Although many of the people in the room knew my story, I would say that approximately half were hearing it for the first time. Brad shared his personal story as it related to my accident, recalling the phone call he received from Jesse. He shared how hard it was to see my broken body when he and his wife Paulette came to visit my bedside only days after the crash. "I'll be honest; Hal looked really, really bad. I mean, you saw the pictures; it was devastating. Doctors didn't even know if he would walk again. Now, even though I knew Hal to be a record-breaker, this was the worst condition I had ever seen any person in during my lifetime, and I was not too sure that Hal would ever be back to normal."

Always one to joke, Brad lightened the mood a little, "Now, I'm sure many of you who know Hal will agree that he's *far from* normal, but I wasn't sure that he would even get back to being the same *weird* Hal again." He went on to tell the inspiring story of the phone call I placed to him from my hospital bed, and how I showed up at Kick-Off Conference to win the fourth place Push Period trophy. "All in all, Hal has set new standards and forever changed the face of Vector Marketing!"

J. Brad continued and based on my experience of watching other colleagues of mine get inducted into the Hall of Fame, I knew the following was coming. "As it is tradition, before I bring Hal up on stage I would like to share *my* letter from Hal's book of letters. Mine is not the typical letter though, rather it is a poem using the letters of Hal's first and last name. Here goes...

I'm sure you are receiving several well-deserved letters of congratulations on your Hall of Fame induction. So, I've decided NOT to write you a sappy, emotional letter. You can never really tell how sincere those kinds of letters are anyway. But poetry, now that comes from deep within the soul! So here is an original poem I call Yo Pal, Is My Pal:

To honor you at this very special time,
I have put together one heck of a rhyme.
To assure you this poem won't be lame,
I've decided to use the letters of your name.
'H' is for HAPPY; that's how you make me feel,
Keep spreading this feeling. You are the real deal.
'A' stands for AWESOME; this describes you.
Your commitment to excellence has always been true.
'L' is for LOVE; I'm not really sure why.
It just seems like that's what 'L' should stand for.
You probably wish that this poem were done,
But I'll have you know, I'm just starting the fun...
Now 'E' stands for the ENERGY that you bring to the table,
If one man can make a difference, I know you are able.
This 'L' is for the leader that you have become,
Do you prefer Mentos or a stick of gum?
'R' means I am REALLY, REALLY impressed,
You have proven yourself to be the best of the best.
This 'O' is for OSTRICH, 'cause it starts with 'O'
There aren't that many good words that start with 'O'.
Finally 'D' stands for DUDE! You DID it! That's DOPE!
I'll bet you could even sell knives to the Pope!
I hope you don't think this poem is lame.
It's my way of saying, 'Congratulations on Hall of Fame.'

Without further ado, please help me welcome onto the stage, my pal and yours, Mr. Yo... Pal... Hal!"

My laughter, caused by Brad's corny poem, quickly subsided, and I took one more glance at my loving Mom and Dad. I smiled proudly and stood up only to find that everyone in the room was already on their feet. Applause filled the large banquet room as I floated onto the platform. Brad extended his hand for a shake, but instead I wrapped both my arms around him and gave him my version of a "Jesse Levine" hug, nearly squeezing the air from his lungs. Overwhelmed with emotion, I had to hold back from planting a big kiss on Brad's face. I placed myself behind the podium and took a few seconds to absorb the scene. Scanning the crowd, I was grateful to see so many familiar faces, so many who had contributed to this moment in one way or another.

"Thank you so much for sharing this honor with me," I began. "Cutco is the best thing that has ever happened to me, and I want to thank the special people that have made it possible for me to be here." I thanked several people in the audience who had been mentors of mine through the years, leaders such as Dan Casetta, Mark Lovas, and Bruce Goodman.

"My Grandma Sally is here tonight," I informed the audience. "I do not think that anyone loves me more than my grandma does. In fact, every single time we talk, she reminds me insistently, *'I love you, Hal. Hal, I love you... Love you... I love you, Hal.'*

I love you, too, Grandma!" I proclaimed.

"Speaking of love, I've spent the last few weeks thinking of what value I could add to your lives tonight—what wisdom do I possess that I could share with you, and if there is one thing that I have learned in my life, it is to love unconditionally. I am not speaking of romantic love, by any means, I've still got a lot to learn in that department... but I am speaking of the love we have for one another.

I believe that the greatest blessings we have are the people we share our lives with, and our greatest joy is in loving each other."

I continued, "But if your love has conditions, or if you tend to judge others before allowing yourself to know them, then I think you might be missing out on something extraordinary. I think that there may be an opportunity for you to grow and to experience infinitely more joy and love in your life.

I have a quote to share with you this evening, and that is, 'Although actions speak louder than words, it is our intentions which reveal our soul.' But it has been my observation that most of us make judgments about other people based upon what they say and do. We deem what people say, and what they do, to be the truth about *who they are.* Take a moment to evaluate whether this observation is true for you—do you judge others upon their words and actions?

Let me ask you a question; by a show of hands, *who here has ever said anything—in the moment—that you didn't really mean? Something that may not have been a true reflection of your character, and you later regretted saying it...? And has anyone ever done something—maybe out of fear, anger, or some other fleeting emotion—that they wished they could take back?"* As I expected, every hand in the room went up in response to both of my questions.

"Would it be safe to say, then, that our words, *and* our actions, don't necessarily tell the whole story of who we are, and who we are striving to become?

The possibility that I am sharing with you is that although our actions may speak louder than our words, neither one of them accurately portrays who we are. I believe it is our *intentions* that speak the truth about who we are. If you desire to create and sustain optimal relationships with the people in your life—to experience true, unconditional love and to be loved in the same way—take the time to get to know people by their intentions. The only challenge is that this takes time, and it requires patience. Sometimes you have to look really deep—five, six, seven layers deep—to know who someone really is… but the reward is priceless."

I paused, holding back tears as I said my final words. "I am eternally grateful for all of you being here to share this moment with me tonight and the value that you add to my life. I truly love each and every one of you for who you are, unconditionally and without judgments.

Thank you."

16

LIVING EVERYDAY LIKE
YOUR LIFE DEPENDS ON IT

*"How you spend your days is the greatest measure
of the who you are becoming."*

—Mark Lovas

I have sold knives like my life depended on it, and it did. This is the greatest lesson I have learned—to live everyday like your life depends on it, because it does. This is the opposite of living each day like it doesn't matter. Each day of your life does matter, because it is who you are becoming in every moment that determines the life you are creating for yourself. In order to truly *LOVE the life you have so that you can CREATE the life of your dreams*, you must do it everyday. There are no time-outs in life, and there is no pause button; *today* is your life. Goals and dreams for the future are vital, but only when they are backed by daily actions consistent with making them into a reality. Otherwise, your goals and dreams are nothing more than fantasy.

For the past seven years—nearly one third of my life—selling knives has been what *I* chose to do, and everything I am today is because of the choices I made every day to be and give my best. It was through unwavering faith and putting forth extraordinary effort each day that allowed me to create the life of my dreams. It wasn't about the knives, the money, or the *Cutco fame*. All of these things brought me joy, but it was the process that defined me. It was the choices I made every single day when I woke up about how I would spend my time. These choices shaped my life and continue to do so.

Looking back, I see that at first I didn't realize my own potential. It was Jesse and other mentors in Vector that saw the potential within me. It was in borrowing confidence from them that I took my first steps toward my desired future. It was in the decision I made on the second day of training to break the *Fast-Start* record—something I had no idea how to do—that my destiny began to take shape. Once I was committed, the *how* revealed itself. And, it was during those instrumental first 10 days of selling Cutco, through my taking action in spite of my fears and failures, that I proved to myself that I could create anything I wanted as long I was willing to commit to the effort. My earlier decision to *take Cutco head on* made it possible for me to take the rest of my life head on as well.

Who I became was the man that, when faced with the greatest challenge of my life, would have the strength, positive attitude and emotional fortitude to take adversity head on. Had it not been for my experience selling Cutco, I honestly do not know who I would have been at the time I was hit by the drunk driver. I cannot promise you that I would have been able to handle such challenge... not physically, mentally, or emotionally.

Upon awakening from my coma after the car accident, for a brief moment I questioned myself. I questioned whether or not I could ever really succeed again. I questioned the validity of my accomplishments. Then I remembered everything that Jesse had taught me and the examples set by my parents. I drew strength from Jesse, my parents, and from my own experiences.

So, what do YOU do? What do you spend your valuable time, energy, and attention on? Is it your career? School? Relationship? Your children? Are you giving your best in every moment? Are you playing from your heart and creating an extraordinary life for yourself and those around you? I hope so. If you are living anything less than your best, I have to ask you, why? What are you waiting for?

Whatever it is that you spend your time doing, *live every day like your life depends on it*, because it does. This is your life—right now—and how you spend it today is the greatest measure of what your tomorrow will bring. You are choosing in every moment. Do not wait another minute to *LOVE the life you have*, for this is the only life you have. And, there is no time more advantageous than NOW for you to take immediate action and *CREATE the life of your dreams*.

It is also time to take full responsibility for YOUR life. By making excuses and blaming other people or circumstances outside of your control, you render yourself powerless to make changes. The moment you take full responsibility for *everything* in your life is the moment you unleash the power to create *anything* in your life.

I could have easily chosen to feel sorry for myself, blamed

others and ended up broke—physically, mentally, and financially broke—living at home with my parents (who would have gladly taken care of me). I could have chosen to blame the accident for my circumstances. I could have proclaimed that it wasn't my fault that my life was the way it was, because it wasn't *my fault* I was hit by a drunk driver. Yes, this could have been the life I chose, the life of a victim. So, why didn't I?

I will tell you why; because no victim *LOVES the life they have*. Victims feel sorry for the life they have; that is the essence of victimhood. And victims do not *CREATE the life of their dreams*; victims wallow in the excuses as to why they cannot. What kind of life would that have been? It was only by taking full responsibility for everything in my life, that I regained my power to create anything in my life that I wanted. I chose to accept my life as it was, decide what I wanted to improve, and then take immediate action toward my vision of the future.

This didn't happen overnight; it took time and it took patience. In fact, it is a never-ending process, and as I sit here writing this to you now, I continue to LOVE the life I have, and with each letter that I type on this keyboard, I am CREATING the life of my dreams. All because I take 100% responsibility for everything in my life... *MY life*. And it is you who must take responsibility for *YOUR life*.

What follows is the *Taking LIFE Head On! Formula* that I have used to *LOVE the life I have so that I can CREATE the life of my dreams*, and it will empower you to do the same.

The Taking LIFE Head On! Formula

How to LOVE the life you have so that you can
CREATE the life of your dreams

Step 1: LOVE Unconditionally

Step 2: Expect the Best—Accept the Rest

Step 3: Be Grateful For What You Have

Step 4: Dream BIG!

Step 5: Take Your First Step

Step 6: Be Accountable To Your Word

Step 7: Surround Yourself With Empowering People

Step 8: CREATE Consistent Progress

Step 1: LOVE Unconditionally

To *LOVE & CREATE*—this is the essence of life. In order to CREATE the life of your dreams, you must first LOVE the life you have. The life you are living NOW is the same life you will be living in the future. Sure, the circumstances that you are going to create for yourself will undoubtedly be different and better than they are now, but it will still be *your* life. As we have seen with so many celebrities who think that they will be happy once they get all the fame and fortune that they want, but then those same celebrities end up turning to drugs, alcohol, or some other vice because they weren't happy to begin with. If you aren't happy with what you've got now, then getting what you think you want isn't going to make you any happier. You must first LOVE unconditionally the life you have today, and then you can begin to implement the rest of the *Taking LIFE Head On! Formula* as a way to *CREATE the life of your dreams.*

I'm talking about loving every aspect of your life this way—without conditions—beginning with your SELF. Love your imperfect self, flaws and all. You are exactly where and who you are supposed to be at this very moment. Love your past, especially your mistakes, because it is by making mistakes that we learn the lessons and establish our values that help us to improve our selves and our lives. Love every past relationship, because it is through your trials and errors that you are becoming precisely the person you will need to be whom your *soul mate* will fall in love with at precisely the time they are supposed to fall in love with you. Love your family, because it is the only one you will ever have. Love your enemies, because they, too, are a part of the grand scheme of your life, and there is a purpose for them being a part of you. Love others despite their faults and shortcomings. Love people, not because they are perfect or because they always know what you want or how you want to be treated. Love them because they are imperfect, just like you. Love them because they only want to do their best, just like you. Love them because they want the same thing that you want—simply, to be happy and to do only what they know to be right. Love them unconditionally, because that is how each of us deserves to be loved. Love what you fear, because the only way to overcome fear is through love. Love deeply, fully, without hesitation or judgment... Love ALL.

Step 2: Expect the Best—Accept the Rest

Deciding on your expectations—what you will choose to expect each day that you wake up—as well as being willing to accept when they are not met, is vital in order to keep moving forward. In life, people get what they *expect*, not what they wish for. This is true in all areas of life and in regards to performance at every level. I don't know too many successful people who wished for success and it showed up at their doorstep, but I know many who expected to be successful and then everything they did—their daily actions—were consistent with their expectations and so inevitably they became successful. The people that you see living extraordinary lives—maybe even lives that you envy—are no different than you or me, they just choose to wake up each day and expect the best from themselves and from life.

Expecting that everything will work out for the best and maintaining an optimistic outlook is a *strategy*, which *usually* results in just that—things working out for the best. Not always, but more often than if you expect that things will go badly, so why not expect the best? This is a strategy for creating a better life. Nobody has *everything* work out for the best, and nobody has everything work out for the worst. But your expectations play a vital role in how things workout overall, so expect the best.

But Hal, what do I do when I expect everything to work out, and it doesn't? As we discussed in chapter nine— ACCEPTANCE is the answer. There are a few things we should consider. First, it's a given that there are things we can control (change) and things we cannot change. Now ask yourself this question: how smart is it to focus your energy on something you can't do anything about, something you can't change? Answer: not very. If you cannot change a circumstance, whether past or present, then accepting it is the only real choice you have.

It has is your wishing and wanting circumstances beyond your control to be different that causes all of your emotional pain. Knock it off! Acceptance is your key to finding peace within yourself and creating a space for emotional well-being and true happiness. Only once we stop resisting reality and accept our circumstances as they are, do we regain control of our lives. Remember to use these three magic words—"CAN'T CHANGE IT"—the next time you find yourself resisting reality. As you say these words to yourself, let the breath flow from your lungs and with it, all of your negative energy.

If you can't change a circumstance, then there is no sense in feeling bad about it. The only logical choice is to accept things as they are, be happy for the sake of being happy, and then decide if you want to make changes. If you do want to change your present situation or future outcome, then take the necessary actions immediately. Of course, as you take these new actions toward your desired outcome… *expect the best.*

Step 3: Be Grateful For What You Have

When you live with an *attitude of gratitude*, nothing is ever wrong. You are choosing to see what you have to be grateful for each moment of every day. Life is as good or as bad as *you think* it is, and it is all a matter of perspective.

Do you see the glass as half-empty or half-full? Or are you an *eternal optimist* like me, and you see the glass as always being 100% full—half filled with abundance and the other half filled with opportunity?

Why is it that the same tragedy can befall two different people, and one sees it as the worst thing that could ever have happened, while the other is grateful for the lesson made available by the experience? Who would you rather be? And whose choice is it whether or not to SEEK gratitude in every moment? It is yours, because there is always something to be grateful for when you choose to find it.

When I wake each day I spend a few minutes in silence, thinking of what I am grateful for in my life. Before I go to bed at night, I do the same thing, reflecting on what I have to be grateful for that day. I strive to maintain my attitude of gratitude at all times, which keeps me grounded, humble, and at peace with all things.

Like I told my friend, Katie, in response to her letter: In life, we all have two pages to look at—one page lists all of our faults, insecurities, and weaknesses, while the other page lists all of our strengths, attributes, talents, friends, family, accomplishments, possessions, possibilities, and everything else we have to be GRATEFUL for. Which page you spend most of your time focusing on is your choice, just as gratitude is a choice... Life, in itself, is a blessing. Choose to be grateful for all that you have.

Step 4: Dream BIG!

In order to *CREATE the life of your dreams*, you must have a clear vision of what the life of your dreams looks like. Know this: anything you can dream, you can achieve, and there is no such thing as a dream that is too big. When you were a child, what did you dream of being, having, and becoming when you were grown up? What has stopped you from living the life that you dreamt of when you were younger? I'll tell you the answer to that—YOU! The only thing that has stood in your way is you.

Most people talk themselves out of the life of their dreams, afraid that they might fail. But YOU are NOT most people! You are extraordinary. You are a dreamer. You are capable of *creating the life of your dreams.* I believe that you and I are kindred spirits—we want more out of our lives, and more out of ourselves, and we are ready to take action!

Do this exercise now: Take out a piece of paper and a pen. Seriously, before you continue reading, grab a piece of paper and a pen. Come on, this part's FUN!

Okay, now at the top of the page write: *THE LIFE OF MY DREAMS.* Before going on to **Step 5** of *The Taking LIFE*

Head On! Formula, set down this book and write down a list of your dreams, everything that you want to:

Have?

Do?

Become?

Share?

Be specific and have fun with this exercise, use it to create a vision for what your life can become, and don't put any limitations on your dreams. Once you have *THE LIFE OF YOUR DREAMS* written down on paper, make copies and hang it on your bedroom wall, bathroom mirror, put it up at the office, etc. Look at it everyday. Take a few minutes each day to vividly visualize yourself driving that car, having the person of you dreams sitting next to you, pulling into the driveway of your dream home. Do you see it? Close your eyes if you have to, and feel what it *will* feel like when you are living the life of your dreams...

Step 5: Take Your First Step

Once you have a clear vision of what you want in your life, you have decided to expect the best and are willing to accept the rest, now it is time to take your first step towards the life of your dreams. This takes discipline.

The journey of 1,000 miles begins with a single step. It just so happens that the first step is the hardest one to take. From my first Cutco phone call, to the first step I took out of my wheelchair, neither of them was easy. But once I took the first step, I was naturally motivated to take the second, the third, and so on. If you can be disciplined to take your first step and then see how you feel, as opposed to getting overwhelmed by the next 50 steps, before you even take your first one, then you will be ready to begin your journey.

I learned a very valuable concept when reading John Maxwell's book, *Failing Forward*... and that is to *act your way into feeling*. Most people do it backwards, hoping to *feel their way into action*. They want motivation to come swoop them up and cause them to feel like doing something, but the reality is that life doesn't work that way. I cannot recall an occasion where I was being lazy on the couch and watching television, when all of the sudden a wave of motivation overtook me and I *felt* inspired to taking action towards my goals. No, it is always quite the opposite; only through my discipline to take action by making my first phone call did I *feel* like continuing and making more calls. It was once I took action that the feeling to keep going came along to my aid.

I'm sure you can probably relate, possibly in the realm of exercise. Can you remember a time when you were laying in bed, sleeping in on a Saturday morning, when out of nowhere you sprung to your feet with an overwhelming passion to go for a run? I doubt it. It is only when you have the discipline to lace up your running shoes—or grab your gym clothes and get into the car with the intention of driving to the gym—that motivation will come alongside and help you out.

If you sit around waiting to *feel like it* before you take action, you are going to be sitting around for the rest of your life. Think of it this way: the toughest part of getting into shape is either lacing up your running shoes or getting into the car to head for the gym. You need only have the discipline to take that first step, and once you take it the *feeling* will come alongside to assist you in completing the journey. When you become a master of taking the first step toward the life of your dreams, you can have, do, and be anything you want. Visualize what you want in your life, and *take your first step* towards your dreams.

Step 6: Be Accountable To Your Word

This I am convinced of: the most powerful force in the universe—that we have access to—is *our word*. When we value our word and live with total integrity—meaning, we do what we say we are going to do when we say we are going to do it, with no exceptions—we become *UNSTOPPABLE*. What would your life be like if you actually did *everything* you said you were going to do, precisely when you said you were going to do it? Then, anything you wanted in your life you could have just by *speaking it into existence.*

Most people do not value their word. They may think they do, but they don't. Consider this: How often do people you know say they are going to do something, and then they don't do it? How often do *you* say you are going to do something and then not do it? Are you ever late to work, school, or when meeting other people? Do you ever cancel plans? Have you ever NOT fulfilled on a commitment because you didn't *feel* like it? Of course you have; we all have. But this does not have to be the way we live our lives.

Unfortunately, finding people who live their lives with total integrity is very rare. It is more likely that you will meet a millionaire than meet someone who does everything they say they are going to do precisely when they say they are going to do it. Imagine what your life would be like if you valued your word like it was worth—not a million—but a billion dollars. Would you be on time if you knew that your showing up on time would earn you a billion dollars? If a billion dollars were at stake, then when you told someone that you were going to do something, would it not be as good as done? So then, why do you not value your word in the same way?

Your entire world transforms when you value your word. All of your relationships—the way people view you—change when you value your word. People respect and admire you, know they can count on you to follow through, but more importantly— YOU know that you can count on yourself to follow through.

So, stop treating your word like garbage and start valuing your word like it is worth a billion dollars. Begin today to do what you say you are going to do, when you say you are going to do it—being accountable to your word, living with integrity—

and you will be joining a group far more elite than the "millionaires."

Step 7: Surround Yourself With Empowering People

Consider this: *we become like the people we spend our time with.* We quickly pick up on their behaviors, habits (both good and bad), language (don't you talk like your friends?), style, ambitions (or lack there of), and just about any other characteristic you can think of. If you wanted to be lazy and live a mediocre life, spending time with other lazy people who are living a mediocre life would probably do the trick. If you wanted to be a drug addict, you probably wouldn't have to hang out with other drug addicts for long before you'd eventually pick up the habit. But if you want to be successful, happy, inspired, living a life filled with love and abundance, then surrounding yourself with people who are committed to the same things is one of the easiest and best ways to set yourself up for success.

Are the people you spend your time with adding value to your life, helping you to *LOVE the life you have* and supporting you to *CREATE the life of your dreams*, or are they not adding much? Are they making it easier to be the best you can be, or do they squash your dreams and tell you to be realistic? And maybe the most important question: is the direction that they are headed in their life the same direction that you want to go? Because if you choose to continue sharing your valuable time with them, then where they end up is probably the same neighborhood you will be living in; how does that look to you?

Am I saying that if your friends aren't on a path toward success, then you should abandon them? And if your family is an unhappy bunch, then you should just disown them? Of course not! I am still close with many of my friends from high school and love my family unconditionally, regardless of how successful or happy they are. What I am suggesting is that you commit to *surround yourself with empowering people*—people who are committed to loving the life they have, creating the life of their dreams, as well as encouraging, supporting, and helping you do the same. Jesse was that person for me, almost from the moment I met him, and ultimately just about everyone in the Cutco company added value to my life in this way. By making the choice to be in that positive environment and surrounding myself with so many empowering people, my success, happiness, and growth were practically inevitable.

We can't choose the family we were born into, but we can choose our friends. We can't always choose where we go to school or where we work, but we can choose which people we associate with in these environments. Choosing to surround yourself with empowering people who are committed to supporting you to *LOVE & CREATE* the life of your dreams will enhance your life more than just about anything else you can do.

Step 8: CREATE Consistent Progress

This is the secret; it is the key to creating the life of your dreams. Once you have a clear vision of what you want, *CREATE Consistent Progress* towards your vision every day until it is real. Some days you may work hard at it, making leaps and bounds, other days you might take only one, small, baby-step forward. Do this, and there is no other option but for you to create the life of your dreams. There is no possibility of failure so long as you *CREATE Consistent Progress*. Eventually success is inevitable, and the only failure would be in giving up.

Do the right thing, not the easy thing. This is a motto to live by that will keep you heading in the direction of your dreams. We are choosing in every moment, so always choose to do the right thing—*CREATE Consistent Progress*—versus doing the wrong thing, which is anything that doesn't move you closer to your goals and dreams. Pretty simple.

Begin today to *CREATE Consistent Progress* towards the life of your dreams, and each day that goes by, not only will you be moving closer, but doing so will become progressively easier with every day that passes. You will replace old habits, such as laziness and procrastination, with your new and empowering habit of *creating progress*. Soon enough, this habit will take on a life of its own, and then you will *be* someone who *creates consistent progress* towards your dreams. It won't take any thought or much effort on your part at that point, you'll just do it out of habit, like brushing your teeth. Your friends, family, and peers will know you as this person, and there will be no turning back; you will be on a mission. I know, because this is who I have become—a *Creator of Consistent Progress* towards my dreams. There is nothing I love more than *to CREATE Progress*. Former pleasures, such as watching television, playing video games, staying up late, sleeping in, and partying are now few and far between. I just don't enjoy them like I used to, and they don't fulfill me because they are not consistent with what I truly want in my life. Why would I sleep in when I can be changing the world? Why would I choose to play video games when I can be reading a book and gaining the knowledge that will help me to be the person I aspire to be? Why would I watch actors on television—actors who are living the life of their dreams—when I can be empowering one of my friends to create the life of *their* dreams? I'm not saying that sleeping in, playing video games, or watching television are wrong, I'm simply relating that these activities do not help me to *create consistent progress* towards the life I have dreamt of.

Don't just *think* about *creating consistent progress* towards your dreams—take action! And don't merely *try* to CREATE *Consistent Progress*—just do it. Trying to do something is about as effective as thinking about doing it—it doesn't move you any closer to your goals and dreams. When someone says, "I'll try" it means the same thing as, *I'll think about it.* "I'll try to be there on time," means that I'll think about being there on time, which really means nothing. So, this final step requires that you take real action towards your goals and dreams, and it requires that you do it consistently, every day.

Live every day like your life depends on it... because it does. Why not make TODAY the best day of your life? Why not make every day the best day of your life? Shouldn't today be better than yesterday, and tomorrow be even better than today?

Most people live their lives with a "someday" mentality and, as a result, do not live an extraordinary life. When you have a mindset that there is always tomorrow, you are not living fully today. You may be letting yourself off the hook today because you think that there is always *someday* to work hard, and to *do the right thing*. I'm sure you give yourself many valid reasons (excuses) as to why you're not creating the life you've always wanted, don't you? I mean, you're probably really busy with work, school, family, your relationship, and you may think it's not important to take your life head on *now,* because you can always do it tomorrow, or next week, or next year, right?

WRONG! What makes us think that we will live any different tomorrow than we are living today?

Start living life to the fullest today, and then you will *CREATE* an exciting tomorrow. There is no someday—*your life is now!* Your life is happening right at this moment and will be determined by the actions you take. Who you are becoming is being defined by the decisions you are making today about how you are spending your time and living your life.

You've made it this far, and I congratulate you on your decision to *take the first step* towards *creating* the life of your dreams by reading this book. And I commend you for your discipline in finishing it to the end. However, this is only the beginning for you and me...

Here we are, with unwavering faith that each day will get better, that *we* will get better. And each day we fight that same fight—the fight to be whole, to be a better person, to do what we know is right—that fight, the human fight. And I'll be the first to tell you: it's not going to be easy. In fact, there would be no reward in the experience of being human if it were easy. But it is worth it. Living every day like your life depends on it is worth it. Loving the life you have so that you can create the life of your dreams is worth it.

I promise you this: *your best story* is yet to come. The life of your dreams, the person that you have dreamt of becoming and everything you've ever wanted is just around the corner, just waiting for you to be committed to creating it.

LOVE the life you have, CREATE the life of your dreams and begin...

Taking LIFE Head On!

Epilogue

THE CHAMPION'S CREED

I AM A CHAMPION

I BELIEVE IT IN MY MIND... I FEEL IT IN MY HEART

I KNOW IT IN MY SOUL

I AM CONFIDENT AND I AM DETERMINED

WHEN THE GAME IS ON THE LINE

GIVE ME THE BALL

I FEAR NO CHALLENGE

I HAVE NO DOUBTS

ANYTHING ANOTHER CAN DO, I CAN DO BETTER

I PRACTICE LONGER AND I PLAY HARDER

I BACK DOWN TO NO ONE—FROM NOTHING

I AM UNSTOPPABLE

I BELIEVE

I AM A CHAMPION

After my accident, I had a breakthrough that changed my life forever, and tonight I want to share my experience with you so that you may have your breakthrough. As I speak to you tonight, you are faced with a choice; you can either hear my words, nod your head, jot a few notes down, go home and go to bed, and wake up tomorrow thinking, feeling, and acting the same as you always do—Or, in the next few moments your entire life can change—Who you are can change, if you will consider my ideas for yourself.

Two nights ago, I was driving home after having had an in-depth conversation with Jesse about one of my heroes, Michael Jordan. Jesse and I are big basketball fans, and we'd happened to be discussing MJ, the kind of player he was, and what made him so special—what made him a *champion.*

On my drive home, I started thinking: what is the difference between Michael Jordan and all of the other players? *What is the difference between Michael Jordan and me?* I pondered what the difference was between people who play the game of life at the highest level—*CHAMPIONS*—and the rest of us who live with the illusion that we are average. The answer became unmistakably clear; at the fundamental level, it is *our thinking* that separates us.

Everything in our lives begins with a thought, and like Henry Ford said, "Whether you think you can, or you think you can't...

either way, you are right." Average people live their lives filled with thoughts of fear and doubt, but CHAMPIONS think on another level. When the game is on the line, and all of the other players are filled with fear and self-doubt, Michael Jordan wants the ball every single time. Why? Because at some point in Michael Jordan's life, he made a decision—one that we can all make—to *think like a champion.*

When most players doubt themselves and their abilities, fear that they will miss the shot and let down their team and the fans, champions maintain unwavering faith that they will make every single shot, even though there is a chance they might miss. If Michael Jordan misses the shot—and all champions miss shots— he has no doubt he will make the next one... and the one after that... and the one after that. It is because he consciously chooses to *think like a champion* that he makes more shots than the average person.

When the game of life is on the line, most of us let our past results limit our present and future results. We let every missed shot, every no-sale—each failed attempt at one of life's tests— further distort our self-concept. The only real thing that separates you from the most successful people in the world is the way that you think about yourself and what is possible for you.

Imagine how your life would be different if you decided to *think like a champion.* Imagine how every day would be different if you pursued everything you ever wanted, even though the possibility of failing exists. So what! The same possibility exists for Michael Jordan, it exists for me, it exists for all of us. What would you attempt if you weren't afraid? Imagine what your life would be like if you took action despite your doubts. What challenges would you take on? It is your opportunity to take control of your thoughts, to *think like a champion*, and begin creating the life of your dreams.

In one night, my life changed forever. I saw what was possible for me—for all of us. I saw who I wanted to be and decided from that moment forward I would never be the same. I had my breakthrough, and tonight you will leave here choosing whether or not you are going to have yours. I plead to you, please breakthrough—break through your limiting beliefs about yourself. They are simply not true. There is nothing you cannot do. Your fears, doubts, and insecurities... none of them are real. They do not exist, only in your mind—*only in your thinking*. On your car ride home tonight, take the first step, and start to *think like a champion*. When you get home, hang the Champion's Creed on your wall, look at it every day, and choose to become... the champion you were destined to be."

*Download your FREE copy of *THE CHAMPION'S CREED* today @ www.YoPalHal.com

I was so full of possibilities!

My baby sister, Amery, looking up at her big brother.

My first Holy Communion at St. Dominics Catholic church with friend, Jamie.

At age 15, DJing Oak Creek Intermediate's junior high school dance and getting help from Hayley and our friend, Jessica.

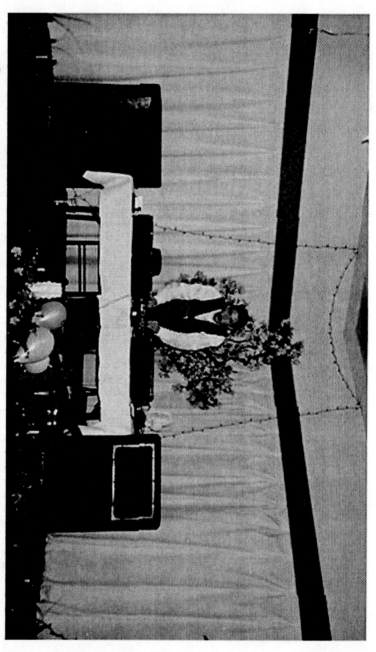

One year later, setting up for a wedding with my new equipment.

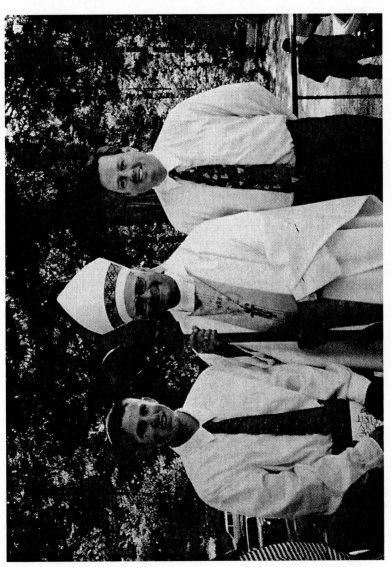

Dad and me with the Bishop on the day of my Holy Confirmation.

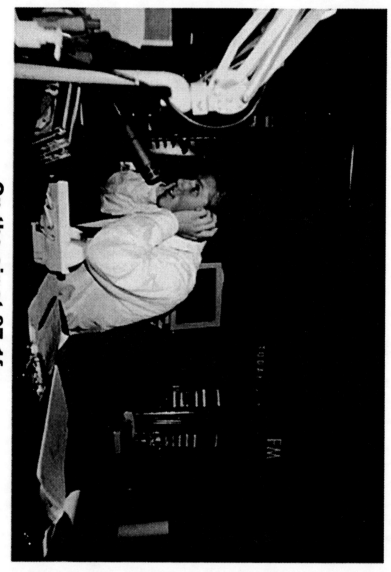

On the air at 97.1fm (sometime between midnight and 6am).

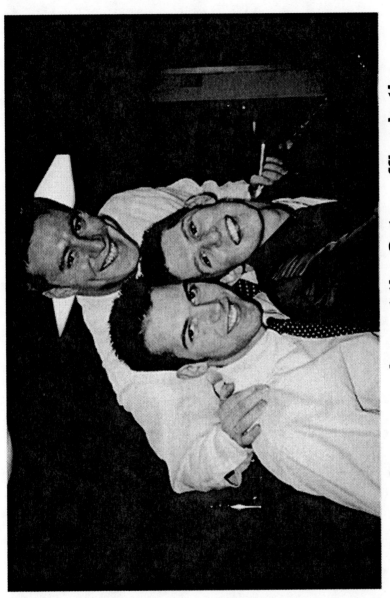

Jesse, Jeremy and me at the Cutco office in the Summer of 1998.

Accepting a Push Period trophy from Bruce Goodman, with Jesse by my side.

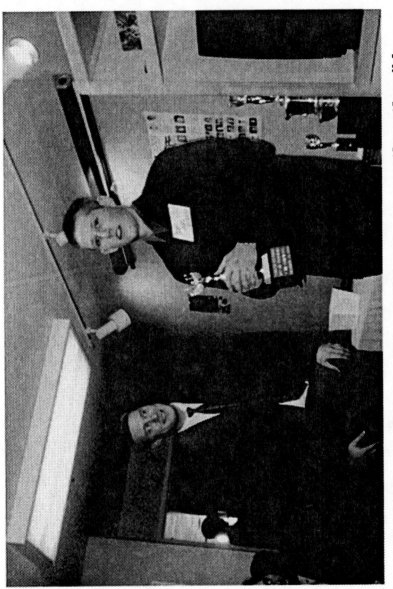

One month before my accident, accepting the #1 Push Period trophy from Jesse.

The front driver's side of the Mustang where the drunk driver hit me.

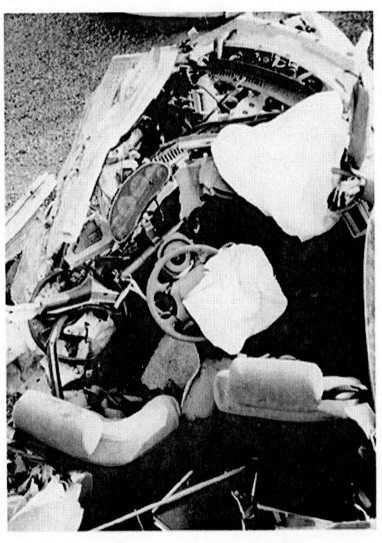

Looking down on my wrecked Mustang.

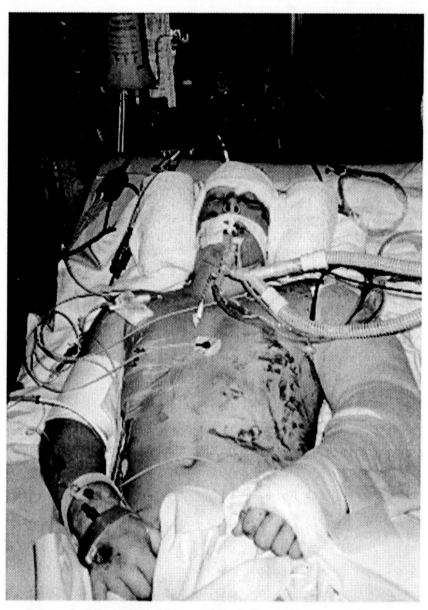

I had 30 pounds of fluids pumped into me in this picture.

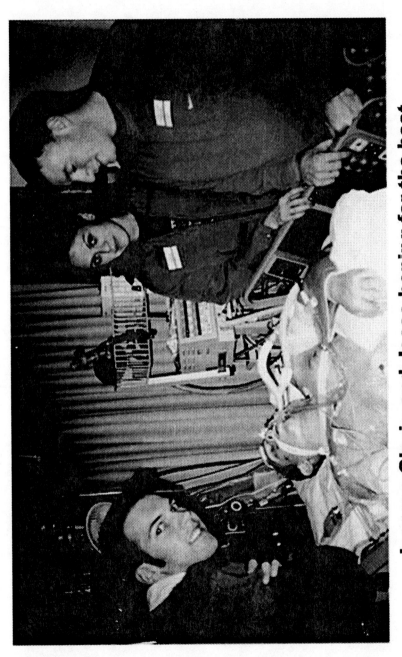

Jeremy, Gloria and Jesse hoping for the best.

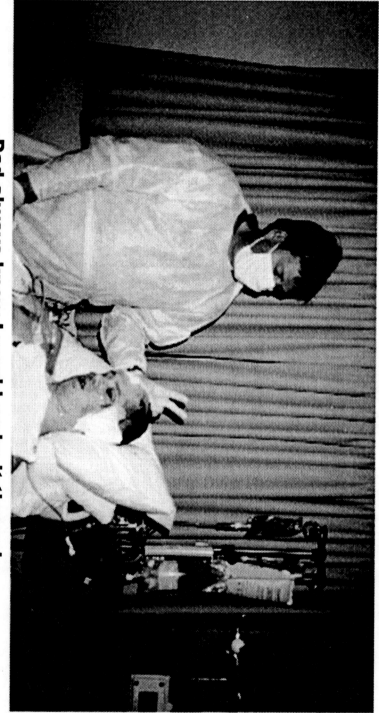

Dad always knew I would make it through.

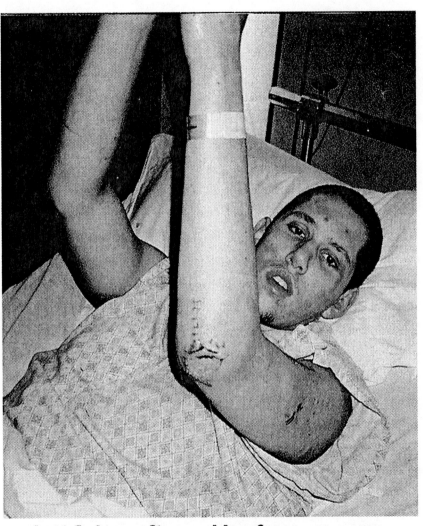

Just 3 days after waking from my coma.

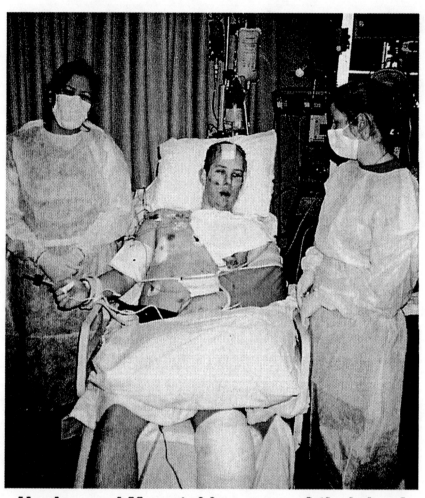

Hayley and Mom taking care of their boy!

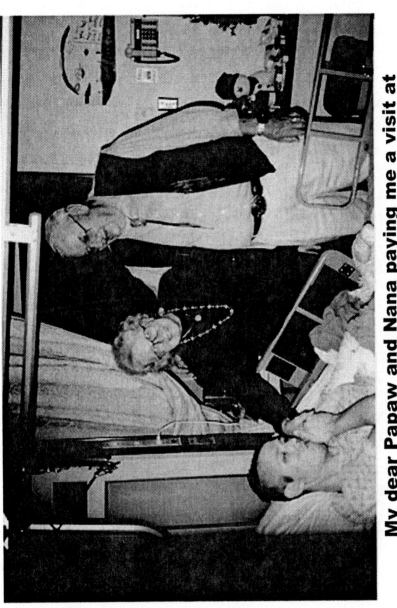

My dear Papaw and Nana paying me a visit at Modesto Memorial Hospital.

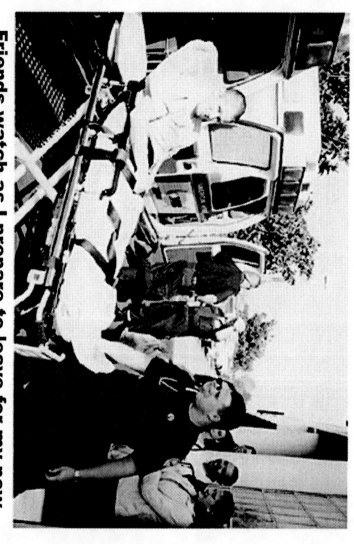

Friends watch as I prepare to leave for my new home at Valley Children's Hospital.

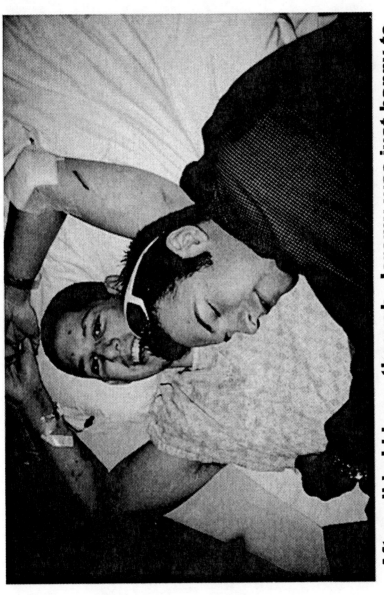

After all he'd been through, Jeremy was just happy to see me alive.

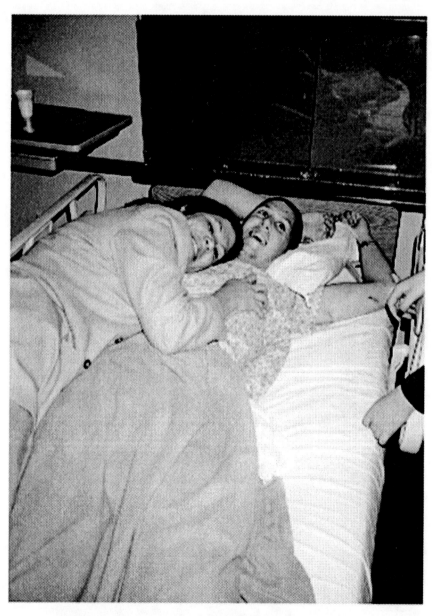

Nobody loves me like my mom!

Miraculously taking my first step with the help of my therapist, Bob, just 3 weeks after the accident.

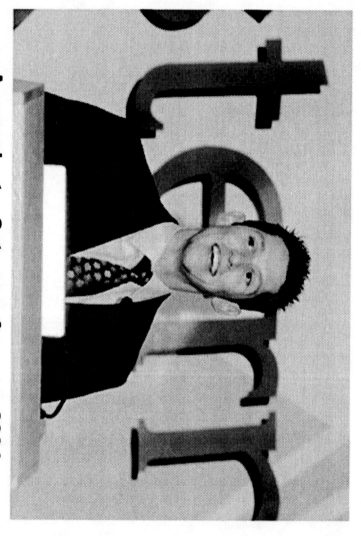

A speech at a Cutco conference, 2004.

Hall of Fame with Dad, Mom, Grandma and Hayley.

VISIT WWW.YOPALHAL.COM TO...

➤ Download your **FREE** copy of *THE CHAMPION'S CREED*

➤ Subscribe to Hal's **FREE** *Life EMPOWERMENT Ezine*

➤ Register for your **FREE** *Life Empowerment Coaching* session with a certified Empowerment Coach

➤ ***Hire "Yo Pal" Hal Elrod to speak at your next event!**

...and much more value to be added to your life!

*If this book has inspired or added value to your life in any way, please share it with others and empower them to *LOVE the life they have so that they can CREATE the life of their dreams.* Copies are available at

www.TakingLifeHeadOn.com

THANK YOU FOR YOUR SUPPORT!

Yo Pal Hal's
Recommended Reading

Reading books will enhance your life and help you to become the person you've dreamt of becoming. I highly recommend that you begin the life-long habit of reading just 5-10 pages each day. The following is a list of books that have added tremendous value to my life and have contributed to the person that I am today.

Awaken The Giant Within, by Anthony Robbins

Conversations With God – Book 1, by Neale Donald Walsh

Failing Forward, by John Maxwell

How High Can You Bounce, by Roger Crawford.

Leading An Inspired Life, by Jim Rohn.

Living Enlightenment, by Andrew Cohen.

Mega Living, by Robin Sharma

Perpetual Motivation, by Dave Durand.

Rich Dad, Poor Dad, by Robert Kiyosaki with Sharon L. Lechter

Self-Matters, by Dr. Phillip C. Mcgraw

The 100 Simple Secrets of Happy People, by David Niven

The Mastery of Love, by Don Miguel Ruiz

The Power of Focus, by Les Hewitt, Jack Canfield, and Mark Victor Hansen

The Power of Intention, by Dr. Wayne Dyer.

The Power of Now, by Eckhart Tolle.

The Rhythm of Life, by Matthew Kelly.

ABOUT THE AUTHOR

Hal Elrod is *America's Empowerment Coach*™ empowering people to LOVE the life they have so that they can CREATE the life of their dreams. Hal has inspired thousands of people with his message over the past seven years, and his mission is to empower millions more as the creator of the *Taking LIFE Head On!*® book series and President of *Global Empowerment Coaching*™.

Hal now thrives in Sacramento, CA, where he is a full-time Life & Business Empowerment Coach, Author, and Keynote Speaker. Also the founder of the *Youth Empowerment Movement*, Hal is committed to transforming our world beginning with the beliefs of our young people.

Hal has recently contributed a chapter about Life Coaching to the upcoming book, *"What's The Alternative?"* (www.WhatsTheAlternativeBook.com), by Dr. Lance Casazza.

Hal's unwavering commitment is to empower you to *LOVE the life you have so that you can CREATE the life of your dreams.*

For more information, visit **www.yopalhal.com.**

Printed in the United States
61166LVS00003B/316-387